The Philosophy of
Anything:

Critical Thinking in Context

By

B.W. Hamby

KENDALL/HUNT PUBLISHING COMPANY
4050 Westmark Drive   Dubuque, Iowa 52002

The Philosophy of
Anything:

Critical Thinking in Context

By

B.W. Hamby

KENDALL/HUNT PUBLISHING COMPANY
4050 Westmark Drive   Dubuque, Iowa 52002

Cover illustration by Dan James

to my teachers and my students, my family and my friends,
and to Julie

AND TO PAUL + AMY

DENNGC + MAYA

AND FOR YOUR FRIENDSHIP + LONG-LASTING

FOR BEST OF LUCK AND BEST

LOVE .

WISHES .

LOVE , B

The function of education, therefore, is to teach one to think intensively and to think critically . . . The complete education gives one not only power of concentration but worthy objectives upon which to concentrate.

- Martin Luther King, Jr.

The Philosophy of Anything:
Critical Thinking in Context
By B.W. Hamby

Contents

Preface

This book, with its flashy cover and audacious title, is *not*, like so many other introductory texts on critical thinking, a textbook on informal logic. That's not meant to be a knock on the usefulness and importance of informal logic, but it has been my experience that teaching critical thinking *explicitly as* informal logic puts most students to sleep faster than mixing cough medicine with quaaludes. This book's effects are hopefully not so soporific. You may therefore applaud now if you are around 18 years old, enrolled as a student in an introductory critical thinking course on a university or college campus, and have bought this book as a required text for that course. I'm confidant that you'll (at the very least) stay awake long enough to make it through this Preface!

Also, this book is not, like so many other introductory texts on *philosophy*, an introduction to that subject's major figures, problems, or history (and although I do not wish to disparage the vast importance of those thinkers, topics, or historical dialogues, either, if you are reading this book in an introductory philosophy course then you may nevertheless applaud here too if you wish).

Instead, in this book I try to set the stage for thinking, by expositing in an accessible an suggestive manner the complicated problems that define some of the most meaningful issues that we encounter in our daily lives. Abortion, global warming, war, capital punishment, affirmative action, illegal immigration, and gay marriage: these are the kinds of moral, social, legal, political, religious, and generally philosophical issues that matter (sometimes very greatly) to us, and about which we have (sometimes very strong) opinions regarding. In the pages that follow, I try to confront a few of these issues in a critical way, in an effort to stimulate and suggest an approach to thinking about them, and to thinking in general.

In some sense, then, while this book is *about* critical thinking and philosophy, more significantly it attempts to be a book *of* critical thinking and philosophy. Instead of just *talking* about what it means to think critically and philosophically, abstractly and from a distance, I have tried to *inspire* thinking in such ways, by actively and concretely engaging the relevant issues of our day in an exploratory and personal manner. My hope is that in doing so I will have pointed out profitable paths of inquiry for those who wish to further explore these issues with a critical and philosophical mind.

What this means, among other things, is that my own feelings about the issues I explore come through, and that I do not try to hide those feelings. It means that this endeavor is my own, and that I try to own it. It means that however much I try to examine these issues taking into account the many different perspectives that are out there regarding them, it is always *me* who is examining them, from my *own* experience, and from my *own* perspective.

It's important for you, the reader, to be aware of this, because otherwise you'll think that I'm trying to be "objective". In other words, you'll think that I'm trying to show and tell everyone the "right" way to think, whatever that means. But this is most certainly not my intention. Actually, I expect many of those who read this book to disagree with my suggestive approach and its results, and I'd like to think that I genuinely welcome their disagreement. This is *part* of what I think critical thinking and philosophy are, anyway: constructive dispute about proper method, and about the conclusions that are reached by that method. Therefore, if what I have written here inspires people to engage, in the spirit of charitable dialectic and open inquiry, the issues in their lives that they attach great importance to, regardless as to whether they see these issues from my point of view, then I think I have succeeded.

Really, then, this book is not a textbook at all, but instead is a convenient *supplement* for textbooks of various kinds. It should be employed to serve as an orienting and exemplifying guide to what every student is expected to do in college, and what every educated person should be able to do in general: Read critically, write critically, and in general, think critically about whatever subject matter they are studying, or whatever issue they are confronted with. In this sense, it matters little what kind of textbook this book ends up supplementing, as the "lessons" contained within it transcend the distinctions between academic disciplines, and apply to *all* intellectual endeavors, on and off campus. It can be used in any setting where a person is learning how to think and write, argumentatively or otherwise. This is one reason why I have appended to the text *actual papers* my students have written. Their thoughts can be used as examples of thinking, and material for critique and discussion.

As I have already alluded to, one underlying and important assumption this book is written in the spirit of (and the one I think it should be *read* in the spirit of) is that *doing* critical thinking is both the means and the end of studying it. Another assumption this book makes is that anyone can learn to think critically about *anything* if they just give their thinking about it some focused and careful attention. While this can mean thinking about critical thinking from a theoretical perspective, as one usually does in informal logic, for me it means *engaging* in critical thinking in a personal, practical, and genuine manner.

This book thus treats philosophy *as* critical thinking, and critical thinking as a way of *doing* philosophy. It tries to show that when people thoughtfully engage themselves in reflective, careful, and conscientious inquiry, and proceed by questioning the very assumptions and foundations upon which they understand various meaningful issues, then such people are in effect proceeding upon a philosophical endeavor. This is not

The Philosophy of Anything

philosophy as history, or as specific philosophical problems, or as the important and relevant thoughts and ideas of (for the most part, brilliant) dead white men; it is not critical thinking as argumentation, or as the study of logical formulas removed from contextual relevance. Rather, it is critical thinking as bare-boned intellectual investigation, and philosophy as open-minded inquiry and personal discovery, concerning important issues of obvious relevance.

Some issues matter so greatly to us and are so relevant that we identify ourselves by them: We are who we are because we feel certain important ways about certain important things. What is *most* important, then (and what can sometimes be very hard to do), is to question the *reasons* we have that *support* the ways we feel about those various issues, thinking beyond merely *how* we feel about those issues in general. We need to make the effort to ask plenty of good questions, and then try hard not to answer any of them too quickly. The "philosophy of anything" therefore means examining our reasons for our beliefs, critiquing them and the opinions that they support; it means thinking critically in the context of issues that matter.

* * *

B.W. Hamby
Oakland, California,
June 2007

Introduction:

The Critical Thinker on Campus

Whatever campus you might be on, you've got to wonder what you're doing in college, after four years in high school, and a lifetime in the classroom. And if you're not on a college campus, and instead you're a high school student, or a college graduate, or a professional, you can (and should) still try to genuinely ask yourself meaningful questions about where you stand at this particular moment in your life. But for those who are reading this book as homework, here are a few meaningful questions you might have entertained, and if you haven't, then you probably should: Why are you here at school, on campus? Do you really want to spend your money on books and classes? Do you really want to spend your time reading and studying? What's the point?

Maybe you think an undergraduate degree will help you get a better paying job than you could get with only a high school diploma? Of course, a Master's degree might get you an even better paying job than you could get with just your Bachelor's degree, and a Ph.D. or an M.D. or a J.S.D. might get you an even better paying job than you could get with just your Master's, so why stop with just a Bachelor's?

Maybe your ambition is to practice medicine, or law, or to teach at a university, and the only way you can qualify for those kinds of positions is to go to college and earn degrees in those subjects; your Bachelor's degree is then just the first step towards some further professional goal. But why do you want to be a doctor, or a lawyer, or a professor? Is it just for the money? The prestige? The vacation time? Aren't there other reasons for choosing a career, and for going to school?

Even if you don't see yourself going on to study more once you're done with your undergraduate degree, there must be some purpose to earning that degree, right? What is it? If you want to support a family, fine. But why do you want a family? If you want to afford to buy a house, great. But why is *that* so important to you? Don't you ever think about *why* you make the decisions you make, *why* the life choices that you choose are so important to you, *why* you believe so strongly in the things you do? Being in college, on campus, do you ever think about why you are here in the first place?

And when (or if) you ever ask yourself these questions, do you ask them in the spirit of *explanation*, merely to *account for* your ideas and beliefs and choices, or in the spirit of *inquiry*, in order to better *understand* why (and whether) your choices and beliefs are *reasonable* or *justified*? In other words, do you ask yourself these questions just to assure yourself with quick answers *that* the choices you make actually make sense, or rather to investigate *how* they make sense; *that* your beliefs can be explained by certain facts, or *why* those facts have influenced your beliefs in the way that they have; *that* your judgments are supported by good reasons, or *whether* the support that your judgments rely upon could be stronger?

As soon as you engage yourself in this kind of rational inquiry, you are thinking philosophically and thinking critically. Not in some abstract, lofty sense that has little personal relevance to anything in your life, nor in some superficial sense that fails to increase your understanding, but in a very concrete, down-to-earth, practical sense that has the *most* relevance to the choices you make and the things you believe as an individual.

Most of us feel so attached to our personal beliefs and the choices we make that questioning them, asking ourselves if they are reasonable, is a painful exercise that we would rather do without. It is to admit the possibility that our beliefs might not be as reasonable as we assume them to be, and that we could at times make better choices. To do this is to admit that we don't have it all figured out, that we know less than we think we do, and that we have more to learn about ourselves and the world. It is, in effect, to admit a certain modesty and humility in the face of things that we take very seriously, and this sort of self-reflection hits very close to home, and is a challenge to embrace. Is it so surprising, then, if most of us fail to reflect in this sort of way?

* * *

Why do this at all, then? If it's so challenging to ask yourself pointed questions about the reasonableness of the things you believe and the choices you make, wouldn't it be easier to just answer those questions in short-shrift, with easy explanations like: "I'm going to college so I can get a job and earn more money than I could without a college degree"? But, why go to college if it's just a means to an end, and the end is a job that you don't yet have, that you could end up never getting, or that you might not even want anymore when you're finally qualified to get it? Is your choice to go to college just about getting a job *after* college and making money? If it is, why? Aren't other things about your experience at school important too? What are they? Why are they important? What in general makes the things you value so valuable to you, and why (or why not) is what you do on campus one of them?

Sure, short-shrift answers that explain your motivations in terms of future goals illustrate that you have some sort of goal-oriented foresight, and that kind of foresight is surely important and relevant if you want (among other things) a career and a family. But if what you're primarily doing in college is getting ready for something else, doesn't that seem like an awfully uninteresting way to live what could potentially be the most interesting years of your life? Wouldn't it be great to use your time on campus to learn and experience new things, meet new people, and increase your understanding of yourself and the

The Philosophy of Anything

world *for the sake of those things themselves,* and not just for some ephemeral future-time that is so far beyond where and who you are right now on campus? And this is certainly not to say that that future time isn't important, and that you shouldn't be goal oriented, but I'm trying to suggest that those future goals might not explain it all for you, and that in order for you to understand what else you might be here for, you might have to ask that all embracing, incredibly important, and frustratingly vague question: "Why?"

But maybe we can be less vague about this whole endeavor of self-reflection, this toilsome task of examining our reasons for what we believe and the choices me make. See, if you're here on campus because your parents expect you to earn a degree, or because of the prospect of a higher wage after graduation, or even because you're looking forward to co-ed dorms and parties on Thursday nights, fine. All these things might explain what you're doing in college, and there might be many more explanations, besides. But what more specifically is the point, if what you're primarily doing is (vainly) satisfying your parents' wish to live their lives through you, or (hopefully) putting yourself in a better position to make more money after you graduate, or (foolishly) seeing how many beers you can drink in one night without passing out? The chances are that you're parents will never be satisfied with your successes because they'll still be disappointed with their own failures, you'll never make as much money as you could spend because there's always something else to buy, and when you try to drink as many beers as possible in one night, you're bound to end up unconscious (or worse) on the floor of a dirty hallway, with a terrible headache and acute dehydration, because after a certain point you'll probably forget how many empty cans belong to you.

The point is, you're here. Yes, perhaps there are various explanations for what you're doing that make perfectly good sense, without having to think too hard about them. It's no secret that this is, after all, a unique environment that you'll never encounter again, offering endless potential for the future; you *know* you should value the moments that you spend here, spend them wisely, and think about the next step. More importantly, however, you should really try to think about and understand the *reasons* that make the next step worth the time, energy, and money you spend here worth it for you, *now*. Now, not later. Now, while you're here. Now, while you're *in it*, regardless of what might come next.

This means, for one, actually reading the books that your professors assign. You're in class, assume that there's something for you to get out of it. Assume that a book or a professor can offer you something, even if it might be a perspective you are unfamiliar with or unused to, and even if it is a position you might disagree with. It also means taking the time you spend in the classroom seriously, as an active, enthusiastic learner. And yes, it means having fun, and being social, and "not letting your studies get in the way of your education," as my Grandfather told me when I started off as an undergraduate. But it also means actively and authentically questioning your choices and beliefs and the ideas you encounter on and off campus, and in and out of the classroom; it means being a genuinely thoughtful person, and

The Philosophy of Anything

striving to better understand yourself, your environment, and the people with whom you interact.

* * *

Now, the flip side of this whole discussion is the reality that many students in their first (and sometimes second and third) year on campus don't have a clue as to what they're doing in college, and any kind of "future plan" is a sort of laughable idea. This is certainly where I stood as an 18 year old, on the University of New Hampshire campus (located just blocks away from the house I grew up in). For such students, college is not about what to study, why to study it, and how best to study it well. It's not about taking classes seriously and authentically questioning why that makes sense. Instead, it's about putting off for as long as possible the reality of working nine to five; it's about living the life of a student, with summers off and parents kept at a distance; it's about finally being independent without having to pay too many bills, or be concerned with all the things that loom on the horizon, in the "real world". And college sometimes feels like this: a dream world set apart from the rat race, a haven for young people in transition, trying to "figure it out", whatever "it" is.

How to think critically, if this is where you stand? What's the point of trying hard at school, if you decide you really don't care about school in the first place? Besides, what if, by the time you graduate, the "it" you thought you had figured out turns out not really to be the "it" you're interested in? Was it a waste of four years, thousands of dollars, and a certain amount of effort, if by the end you still don't know what kind of job you'll get after graduation, or you still don't have an answer to that infamous question: "what will you do with *that* degree?" Why bother deciding, then, when these doubts seem so palpable, and the future is so uncertain?

Not only do current students feel this way, but here's where a lot of college *graduates* stand, asking themselves if it was worth it, wondering what to do now that the real world is at their doorstep. And this is the reason why college should be more than just vocational training. This is the reason why it should be more than just preparing workers for the work place. And yes, it is the reason why there are (unfortunately, but understandably hated by most students) *general education requirements*. The idea is that your education goes beyond just some "major" subject you may (or may not) want to focus on, beyond the particular skills you'll need for a job once you graduate, beyond questions of career and future goals. Instead, general education requirements illustrate how your education is firmly anchored in the present moment, in your *life* as a student and as a thinking person.

The idea is that college is more than just career planning. Because the skills that transcend the specialized ones you'll use in whatever job you get are the skills that you learn by being exposed to the wide variety of learning that is out there, and the ones you'll use in your daily life, on and off the job. They're the skills that enable you to use your mind to any purpose, at any time. If you're not trying to become a scientist, for instance, it still behooves you as an educated person to know what a scientific theory is, and how science is different from scientism. If you're

The Philosophy of Anything

studying math, it's still important, quite apart from your skills as a mathematician, for you to be able to read some piece of literature or some newspaper editorial, or to watch the news, and think and write and speak about what you read or see in a constructive, illuminating, and intelligent way. General education requirements, in other words, exist to expose students to the different aspects of what it means to be a thinking person. They exist to foster multidimensional intellects, people who are intellectually competent in general, and not just in some focused disciplinary perspective, specifically.

College, then, especially at "Liberal Arts" institutions, should be about education, of course, but the education of the *whole person*, and an education directed towards a diversity of meaningful objects. The word 'education' itself derives its meaning from a related word in Latin, *edūcĕre*, meaning "to lead forth". The idea is that we contain an immense intellectual capacity that has yet to be realized, and that we have a great native potential to realize an increased knowledge and understanding of things and ourselves. It can apply to the subject at hand by indicating the notion that your time in college is less about facts being put into your head, and more about a wide range of skills being developed from capacities that you already somewhat possess. Your education on campus then is about exposure to new ideas, but it is also about exposure to new ways of learning. So, when you approach the variety of classes that you inevitably will take as an undergraduate, the one constant is that you will always be approaching them from your own personal perspective, and your own latent capacity, even if you are being asked to approach them in other different and more formalized ways than you are used to.

Thinking about the word 'education' can help us to orient ourselves to what an undergraduate education is all about because it implies that the knowledge and understanding we seek is not "out there" in the external world, and that it is not just a matter of somehow cramming information into our brains in sufficient quantities with the hope of retaining that information so that we can pass a final examination. Instead, it implies that what we "bring to the table" in our education is essential to the new things we can learn, and the new ideas with which we can acquaint ourselves. This means that who you are, what you believe, and the choices you make, *matter* to what you learn, how well you learn it, and *what you end up doing with that learning.* Your education is in every sense of the word a personal and practical endeavor, with personal and practical consequences.

* * *

Here is where this book comes in. How can you make your education, not just on campus, but throughout your life, a personal, meaningful, constructive endeavor? Concerning the things that are relevant and matter greatly to you, how can you understand them better, and support your positions on them in the best, most thorough manner? My answer is this: to charitably consider other ways of thinking about those things, to honestly and critically examine your own way of thinking about them, and to ask questions that frame those issues in illuminating ways, teasing out and making concrete their deep and complicated meanings.

So that's what this book will try to facilitate: a critical investigation of meaningful and contentious issues, like moral certainty, abortion, and war. By asking questions, not in an effort to finally answer them, but in an attempt to better understand the issues themselves, we can educate ourselves about things that really matter to us. Chapter One will try to orient us to the foundational question of our moral certainty, and the reasons why we sometimes think we are justified in believing in the things we believe and acting the way that we act. Chapter Two will investigate the issue of abortion, outlining the different questions and approaches to thinking about that most divisive of issues. Chapter Three is about war, and also examines the questions and reasonings concerning that very current and relevant issue. Finally, the Conclusion (which very well could be read at any time) will briefly summarize where we stand as thinkers concerning these subjects, and will point to the possibility of further study, after we have left our classrooms on campus, concerning the fundamental intellectual endeavor of thinking critically and philosophically. Appended to these chapters are two sections that contain students essays, and a section with suggestions for further reading, organized according to the subject of each chapter.

In the future, I hope to add more chapters, exploring some of the other meaningful and relevant issues we are confronted with today, but an important thing for anyone who reads this book to understand is that any issue can be approached from the spirit of charitable inquiry; the issues I choose to approach here are merely ones I am very interested in, which affect me significantly, and which I think are interesting to and affect others significantly as well. This book, again, tries to inspire a movement towards examining the *reasons* we have that support the positions we believe in, and the actions we perform. What it hopefully accomplishes is a suggestion of and invitation to thinking critically about particular things that matter to us, so that we can then think critically about anything. With that, let's begin.

Chapter One:

Thinking Critically about Moral Certainty

How can we be certain that the positions we hold regarding the issues of great importance to us are the *right* positions? Furthermore, how can we be sure that the positions that others hold are right or wrong? What about our actions? How are we to judge the moral status of the things we do? But what do "right" and "wrong" mean, anyway, and how can we be certain of our position on *that* issue? By "right" do we just mean "correct", as in "politically correct" or "socially correct", or correct according to our religion, or do we mean something else? What if what is correct is just what is socially acceptable? Are moral standards then unable to transcend societal norms and refer to something universally true, beyond our cultural conventions?

These questions begin to illustrate the idea that before we can profitably investigate issues regarding specific moral dilemmas, we need at least to begin investigating what our standards or rules for morality are in the first place. In other words, we need to be able to think about the principles that make something right or wrong, why those principles make sense, and how other competing principles measure up to them. After all, how can we constructively investigate whether a woman has a right to her reproductive freedom, or whether war is just, or whether it is right to execute someone who has committed murder, if we don't have some measure by which we can judge these moral dilemmas, or if we haven't even begun to examine what that measurement might consist of?

Having said that, however, while in this chapter I try to *frame* the fundamental question of moral standards in the context of our moral certainty, *suggesting* some of the aspects of that question that make it so complicated, I do so without really trying to *answer* it at all. I'll not pretend that an issue like morality can be definitively answered in the space of one short chapter of a small college text, or even definitively answered at all for that matter. In our posing of meaningful and complicated questions we should not expect to answer them too quickly. Keep that in mind as you read on.

But if we can't get a final answer on this topic, why bother exploring it? Furthermore, what's the point of trying to illuminate specific moral dilemmas, if our justification of the moral standards that we use to evaluate those dilemmas remains unclear? My only response is that philosophy, you will find, is often like this: we are

The Philosophy of Anything

compelled to ask fundamental questions that have a far reaching impact on other questions, but "answering" those questions, in the sense of ending the discussion on them, never really happens. Some people find this incredibly frustrating, but those who are used to investigating things philosophically are somehow able to accept the complicated nature of the things that they investigate, embracing the lack of finality that those investigations yield. They understand that whatever such investigations lack in finality, they make up for in increasing our understanding of the issue at hand, by enabling us to see an issue's many different sides, and its many different implications concerning other relevant questions.

This is especially true of an issue like morality: a perennial (and perhaps exclusively) human concern that we, as humans, have been aware of and confounded by for literally thousands of years, and that has a far reaching impact on anything else one cares to name. But again, just because it is confounding doesn't mean we can't understand it better, and it doesn't mean in that trying to understand it we can't learn something about it and its far reaching implications. In fact that is just what I hope to accomplish in this chapter: to suggest some paths of inquiry that might prove fruitful in helping us understand some of the questions that are involved in justifying our moral judgments. And so I choose to focus on our feelings of moral certainty regarding our justifications for different moral standards.

* * *

To recapitulate: if we are already to some extent certain of the moral status of our actions and beliefs, and we are certain of what in general constitutes right and wrong and what specifically makes those actions and beliefs right or wrong, then how can we justify that certainty, and the various other positions of ours that we attach it to? How do we judge actions and beliefs, our own and those of others? According to moral rules? According to religious doctrine? According to social norms? Do we judge them based upon legal standards? Why, then, do those legal rules proscribe some things, but not others? Why do they require this, but not that? Aren't our laws based upon some sort of moral principle? If so, we have to ask what moral principles lie behind our laws. The same goes for our religious commandments: what, *besides* that fact that some authority (like a priest, or God) says that something is right or wrong, makes it so? If we do not admit that there are some reasons behind moral judgements, then must we admit that the moral standards we hold are based upon some unknown, unconscious, or unexamined prejudice? Should we even judge our values at all, or can we get away with our moral stances on particular issues boiling down to an unexamined position on what makes something moral in general? If so, is our certainty just a matter of feeling? Are our moral judgments and our stance on what constitutes the best standard of right and wrong just as dogmatic as our judgments about why we go to college, or our judgments about why some things are more or less important to us than other things, or our judgments about anything else?

What if, to look at this issue from another perspective, morality is just a matter of self-interest, and the feelings of others matter only insofar as they have an impact on you? But this is surely a manner of judgment that constitutes some standard itself. Why should we think that self-interest is the best way of making moral judgments? On the other hand, should a correct moral standard place less emphasis on an individual, and more importantly consider the effects on groups of people considered as a whole? Why is this a justifiable or unjustifiable standard?

But maybe all this talk of justifying our moral standards and our moral certainty is just a waste of time. Maybe there isn't any such thing as a correct moral standard to begin with, and our moral certainty is an artificial construction that has no objective meaning. Is morality just a figment of our imagination, something that we have strong intuitions about, but that has no truth or rational basis? If our project in this chapter is to begin to examine what constitutes our moral beliefs and the moral status of our actions, if we're asking what it means to justify those beliefs and actions, then doesn't it make sense to ask whether our moral certainty can ever really *be* rationally justified in the first place? What if there's no such thing as a rationally justified standard?

These very basic and very fundamental questions relate to everything we think and everything we do, and form the basis of who we are as individuals. Morality, in other words, whether you believe in it or not, and whether you believe one thing about it or another, is truly a central question that we must confront if we are to be genuinely thoughtful people. The remainder of this chapter consists of a further discussion of our moral certainty, framed in light of one very well-known and challenging position, and one not so well known position: moral relativism, and moral skepticism, respectively.

* * *

We often hear people speak, and many of us often find ourselves speaking, of the "relative" quality of the actions and beliefs that we call right or wrong. What people usually mean by this is that the standard by which people make justifiable moral judgments is different for different people. For instance, in some cultures it is permissible for a man to have multiple wives. In others it is not permissible. These are culturally relative circumstances. In the United States and in many other countries, those who make more money are taxed more. Those who make less money are taxed less. These are economic-class relative circumstances. Some would say, however, that having more than one wife is morally wrong, in every circumstance, regardless of the different standard that some cultures have for judging this matter. Similarly, there are those who believe that regardless of a person's economic class, everyone should be taxed the same.

If we accept relativity does that then mean that we must not place some standards of moral judgment above others as being more justifiable and therefore more true, and some below others as being less justifiable and therefore less true? In other words, if we accept moral relativism, must we accept that all standards stand on equal ground, and that judging them in relation to each other is a futile exercise, incapable of yielding relevant knowledge or understanding? If this is the case, and value judgments have no universal truth, what are the consequences for our judgments about the things we care so deeply about? How convincing is moral relativity, anyway, and should we accept it as our guiding moral principle?

As an aside to all of these perplexing questions, it should be remarked that it seems that whatever we say of moral relativity, moral *certainty* is certainly a psychological fact. It is a commonplace phenomenon that people are often very sure of the moral status of their actions and their beliefs, and that this certainty is at odds with the certainty of others. We see evidence of this almost everywhere we look: anti-war demonstrators picketing the White House, demanding that the President bring the troops home from Iraq, contrasted with the President himself, uncompromisingly adhering to a "stay the course" policy in a civil war that his policy helped to create; pro-choice advocates, lamenting the recent Supreme Court decision that proscribed a certain type of abortion procedure (more on this in Chapter Two), contrasted with pro-life advocates, hailing the same decision as a victory for unborn life; volunteers giving their time in service to a non-profit organization dedicated to decreasing gun violence, contrasted with donors to the National Rifle Association; the feeling of guilt most of us have experienced that leads us to apologize when we feel we have done harm to someone else, contrasted with the self-righteous attitude of some who refuse to apologize because they believe they have committed no wrong. The list could go on and on, and all are examples of the certainty that people feel concerning the moral status of their beliefs and actions, whether those beliefs or actions they believe to be either right or wrong, and all are examples of conflicting certainty relative to each person's views. Many of us, then, much of the time, implicitly and pre-reflectively, are quite certain of the moral status of the things we think and do, even (and perhaps especially) in light of the fact that others disagree.

Now, this is not to deny that moral *uncertainty* exists too. Just as we can point to a seemingly endless number of examples of people who are unequivocally assured in the moral status of their actions or beliefs, so too can we easily point to those people whose actions or beliefs, from their own perspective, fall into some gray moral area, and who admit that they are unsure as to whether what they believe or what they do is right or wrong. Sometimes, also, we can be sure of something one moment, then unsure of it the next, or sure of one thing, but not of another, or just plain unsure of most of the things we find ourselves confronted with.

Perhaps this state of psychological uncertainty concerning the moral status of our actions and beliefs is even more common than that of our certainty regarding what we think and do. Or perhaps it is the result of our reflection on our actions and beliefs, and only occurs when we genuinely recognize the complicated matter at hand. Perhaps our uncertainty highlights the certainty that we sometimes feel, and points out the possibility of different moral perspectives.

* * *

At this point I feel I should point out an important aspect of the language I have used to frame this issue of our justification of moral standards and our moral certainty. That is, this whole time I have speaking about our moral *beliefs* and our moral *actions* as if they were one and the same thing. Or at least I have been mentioning them together, implying that they have the same importance when engaging the topic of morality. And while they have a lot in common, we have to realize that there are very significant differences between them. They are not, then, synonymous, regardless of how we feel they somehow relate to one another.

Some believe that it is impossible to talk of moral actions without talking about moral beliefs, and some believe that moral beliefs, since they do not directly impact others in the way that actions do, matter very little when compared to the actions and behavior that has an effect, for either good or ill, on others. For this reason we often isolate one or the other when we talk of our moral standards, because to do so makes our judgments about them more focused. In other words, if we restrict our discussion to actions, or to beliefs, then we can avoid talking about how one influences the other, and so can hone in on what makes some right action right, or some wrong action wrong, for instance.

This is another debate within the issue of what justifies our moral standards. That is, we need to ask whether those moral standards are standards according to which we judge actions, or according to which we judge beliefs. Are our standards different if we use them to judge the people who have those beliefs, and perform those actions? For my purposes here, though, I'll lump actions and beliefs together, and proceed knowing full well that such a discussion could take up our whole time. But just one more word on this side-issue before I resume talking about moral certainty and relativism.

One thing to notice about the issues that this book tries to present is that the relevance of each issue extends far beyond merely how we feel about it. For how we feel about something is intimately related in every case with things that actually happen concerning it, apart from our feelings about it, and apart from our thoughts about it. In other words, abortion is wrong for someone who is pro-life, not just because they feel that the idea is wrong, but because for such a person *actually performing an abortion is wrong*. There is an *action* involved, and this action pro-life advocates would claim is wrong. *Of course* they *believe* it to be wrong, but the "it" they believe to be wrong is an *action* and not a *belief*.

This might seem quite obvious. Actions are different from beliefs. But what is the difference, and how interrelated are they? Well, first of all, people have beliefs, and people perform actions. But judging a person's actions is different from judging a person's beliefs, because a belief doesn't always have an effect out in the world, whereas that is just exactly what an action is. Also, judging a person's actions or beliefs in turn is different from judging just the person himself or herself. But presumably, a person's actions most of the time cannot be so easily separated from their beliefs. And if their beliefs are intimately tied to who a person is, then maybe we can make some moral judgment about a person according to their actions as well as their beliefs.

The Philosophy of Anything

But all this, however it may seem true, is still just talk of psychology, about our states of mind, and our strong feelings about things. While this is an interesting question and topic, it is much more interesting to proceed beyond the psychological and ask, whether, *given* our moral certainty regarding things that we believe are either right or wrong, are we *justified* in that certainty? In other words, what about our certainty makes us believe that the answer is quite apparent, and could not be anything but? What are the *reasons* we have that support our certainty, and what reasons do we have that might call that certainty into question? As a corollary, what leads to our *un*certainty, and makes us think that the answer is not so easy as what we might at first think on the face of it?

Few of us, if we are being intellectually honest, can truthfully say that we are morally certain about every issue that we are confronted with in our lives, even if some of us might feel certain about many issues. For most of us, though, there are at least a few issues, beliefs, and circumstances that give us pause, and make us wonder what is really wrong or right. In other words, for however much we feel certain about some things, we also feel uncertain about others.

What is important then, is again, not just asking whether or not we are certain about the moral status of what we believe and do, but asking about what reasons *make us* certain or uncertain. We might say that we *know* what right and wrong things are, but what is it that makes them right or wrong, and more importantly, why are we certain that those reasons for calling something right and calling something wrong are the *best* reasons for calling them such? Again, what justifies our certainty in matters of morality? This is one of the most difficult things to figure out, and most of us stop trying, once we realize how difficult it really is. Most of us don't want to spend our time thinking about these very tough questions, because it's easier just to pretend that we have them figured out. But we don't have it all figured out. When we confront the issue of our moral certainty, and what constitutes a convincing moral standard, anyone who bothers to give the question any kind of focused attention realizes that whatever intuitive answers we might quickly come up with, they are almost always, without fail, not nearly so easily well-justified. At the very least our certainty regarding what we consider to be right and wrong can be questioned and penetrated in such a way that we afterwards might not feel so certain about our position anymore.

Although many of us proceed in our lives upon the assumption that we are justified in our moral stances, and indeed, although perhaps we *must* proceed in such a way, so as to make society at all possible, nevertheless, if we examine our reasons for why we feel certain about the moral choices that we feel certain about, we will find that none of those reasons stand up absolutely to criticism. In other words, despite the necessity of our beliefs about morality, our certainty regarding those beliefs is actually unjustified. This is to say that the reasons we have that make us certain about issues of morality do not adequately answer the criticisms that are always possible to be leveled against those

The Philosophy of Anything

reasons. This is not necessarily to say that it is impossible to adequately answer them, but rather that we haven't as of yet answered them with sufficiently adequate answers so as to preclude any further questions being asked regarding them. Maybe this means it is impossible to answer them, maybe not, but if you study the question of morality at all, you'll see how very difficult it is to find a moral theory that cannot be called into question by some careful and critical examination.

If this is true, then some would say it has some very crucial and far reaching consequences for our lives. It means that although we often *act* as though what we do and think has some sort of certain moral quality, we can never *actually* (which is to say rationally, justifiably) be certain about what that moral quality is. It means that despite our reasons for thinking or doing some things, and our feeling that those things are truly right or wrong, those reasons are never justified enough for us to be absolutely certain about them.

Some would say that this leaves us in a very precarious position, socially and culturally. If we are never justified in being morally certain, some would claim, then that gives us license to do anything we wish, regardless of any kind of moral checks or balances. If nothing is 100% morally certain, than anything goes. But this conclusion does not necessarily follow from accepting the premise that our moral certainty is ultimately unjustifiable. After all, most of us, even if we were to grant that our certainty cannot be defended in an air-tight way, would have to point out that our intuitions in these matters still exist for *some* good reasons, despite the ultimately unjustifiable character of some of those reasons, and that those intuitions about the reasons for our moral stances are meaningful, and should be followed, even if they cannot be *proved*, like a mathematical equation, as being correct. For example, most of feel that murder is wrong. When we try to examine why we think this is so, we might be confronted with conflicting perspectives, but usually we still retain the strong intuition that murder is wrong. This is to reiterate the point that we still have decisions to make, and that we still believe things, even if those things we do and those things we believe have no ultimate justification for why we do them, or why we believe them.

Is this like having your cake and eating it too? Maybe. There's something pretty confusing about saying that our moral judgments are never justified, but that it's okay to *act* as though they are. There's something problematic about saying we can never prove that what we think is right or wrong is truly right or wrong, but we should nevertheless investigate our reasons for those beliefs anyway.

In order to determine whether this thesis is correct, whether no justification for our moral certainty is good enough, we would obviously have to identify and evaluate all our justifications for our moral certainty, including what morality is in the first place. In other words, every moral standard would have to be examined, and all the reasons for and against each would have to be weighed. Then we would have to compare them all, and see which reasons do their job better than others, and which do their job best. If any of these justifications can stand up to criticism fully, then the thesis is disproved. Of course, we would have to figure out what "stand up to criticism fully" means, and then we would have to spend the very laborious process of actually evaluating all the moral justifications we could find, and this, again, is far beyond the scope of what this chapter tries to do. It's even far beyond what one person to do, given a lifetime of research and scholarship. The problem of what is a satisfactory justification is perhaps the hardest question of morals. Instead, then, I will end this chapter by very briefly returning to the topic I mentioned at the beginning of it, and will examine the justifications for one type of standard by which moral certainty is sometimes determined by people, and which presents a significant problem for the topic as a whole: moral relativism.

* * *

Often times, when talk of values and the attendant disagreement that usually comes along with that kind of talk arises, relativism is a sort of wall that stops conversation from proceeding. "It's all relative. Who are you to say what is right and what is wrong, when people in different cultures feel so strongly about what they do, and all you can point to is that we, in this culture, feel differently?" How can we respond to such a challenge?

Here's an example: If an American who is a feminist (meaning a person who believes that men and women should have equal rights and opportunities) is talking about how he thinks that it is wrong for women in Muslim dominated societies to be forced to cover their faces and bodies, and how genital mutilation in some African countries is abhorrent, then someone might easily reply to him: "Sure, our society and culture here in the United States tells us that those things are wrong, but those other cultures say that those things are okay, and even desirable and obligatory, so who's to say which social perspective is right and which is wrong?"

How can we reply to such an objection? It's true after all: Our society *does* tell us that some things are right, and some things are wrong, that, to use the above example, it is wrong to mutilate a girl's genitals, and that it is right to allow woman the freedom to choose what they wear and how they wear it.

But wouldn't some American feminists want to reply that genital mutilation is wrong, period? It is wrong, not just because our society thinks it is wrong, but it is wrong because it is wrong *in principle*? It is wrong because to mutilate a girl's genitals causes her physical and emotional harm, for instance. And causing a person physical and emotional harm is impermissible. It is impermissible, not just for Americans, or westerners, but impermissible, period. Furthermore, genital mutilation is wrong because the victim does not have a say in having it done to her. And individuals should have control over what happens to their bodies. This too, the feminist might claim, is a value that transcends social norms. Finally, genital mutilation is wrong because when you mutilate a person's genitals, you are not treating them as a dignified member of the human race. And women and especially girls should be treated equally and with respect, and recognized as being human. This principle too, goes beyond merely some cultural perspective.

One problem with relativism, as the above example illustrates, is first of all, that we do not just appeal to our society's standards as the reason for what makes something right or wrong. The reasons why genital mutilation is wrong, as we saw that the American feminist might claim, are wrong in all societies, and in all situations, not because they are wrong in this society, but because they violate principles that transcend cultural contexts. The case is the same for *right* actions. If you see someone drop their wallet, it doesn't matter what country you are in, or what country you come from, there are reasons why it is usually right to pick that wallet up, and return it to its owner. Again, the reasons that make such a action right transcend the fact that our culture might deem it to be so, and rely upon the idea that moral standards are true because they are true, and not because a society says they are true. In the case of the dropped wallet, this standard is something like the golden rule: you should return the wallet, because you'd want the wallet returned to you if you dropped it. I'm not trying to say that the golden rule is the correct moral standard that we should judge everything by, but I'm pointing out that this appeal to a universal moral standard is the hardest hurdle, I think, for a justification of moral relativism to clear.

It should be noted here that maybe there isn't in fact a universal standard that we can appeal to that goes beyond what our culture tells us is right or wrong. Maybe a moral absolute is just wishful thinking. But many of us act as if there is such an absolute, so it would be helpful if this is something we investigated. Since we often find ourselves appealing to reasons that justify our moral stances on issues that go beyond merely what our society tells us is right or wrong, this represents a challenge to relativism.

Another related hurdle that relativism has to deal with is the idea that despite a society's moral norm, that norm might be rejected by people within a society. Who then, decides what a society deems morally permissible, or impermissible? The question becomes even more complicated when we ask what society tells us we must do, or what it tells us goes beyond what we must do.

Take another example. Today American society is dealing with an issue that sees people deeply divided along religious, political, and social lines: gay marriage. Should gay people be allowed to get married, or not? People on either side of this issue will give their reasons for why they feel the way they do, but one reason that makes very little sense to give, for instance, on the side that would like to see gay marriage proscribed, is that not allowing gay marriage is the societal norm. After all, this is the contested issue in the first place: What is "normal" in this society is just what is being called into question! Of course gay people aren't allowed to marry in most states. But *should* they be allowed to? If they shouldn't be allowed to, the reason obviously can't be that they aren't allowed to. You'd then be arguing in a circle. Many people feel that gay couples deserve the right to marry each other if they choose, despite the fact that the culture that they live in is predominately on the other side of the issue. But just because a majority feels one way and a minority feels another, doesn't mean the majority is right, and the minority wrong. What is morally correct or incorrect should not be decided democratically, it should be decided based upon the reasons that someone can provide that justifies what makes something right or wrong. How many countless morally reprehensible things that we as a society used to sanction were overturned as being the morally reprehensible things they were, all in the face of overwhelming societal resistance? You can list them off quite easily: slavery, racial and gender discrimination, child labor, blacklisting, etc. etc.. The point is, convincing moral standards do not always conform to a society's moral norms. People within societies disagree with the standards of their own societies, and this is something that moral relativism does a poor job accounting for. This goes back to something I mentioned at the beginning of this chapter, and that is the idea that our moral standards are more than just our laws. When something is illegal it is illegal for a reason, beyond just the fact that a lot of people think it should be illegal. The rules that govern our society, in other words, are not arbitrary: they must somehow be able to be justified by reasons that go beyond our societal norm.

* * *

I have just, in a very brief manner, laid out some thoughts about our moral certainty, our moral standards, and how we can begin to think about these important issues. Have I answered any of the difficult and fundamental questions that revolve around morality? No. For some, this will appear as a serious shortcoming of my effort to elucidate this issue. But hopefully, I *have* accomplished what I explicitly set out to do, which was to get you to think about this issue, and introduce meaningful questions that might help you to think about it further.

The problem of justifying moral standards is an issue that we cannot avoid if we are to think philosophically, and think critically: It permeates every issue, and forms the basis of who we are, as individuals and as societies. But the only answer we have found concerning this all important issue is a realization that the answers will be very hard to come by, if they come at all. Nonetheless, I encourage those of you who are reading this book to continue to think about what it means to be morally certain, especially in the context of the issues that matter to you, and especially in the context of what it means to offer reasons that support your certainty regarding those issues.

If you are convinced of the importance of *this* issue, and if you recognize how deep questions of morality take us, I'm sure you can imagine that the literature that has been written on it is immense. Therefore, if you're interested in actually studying the philosophy of morals, I suggest you take an introductory class in ethics: in it, you'll study the different standards that have been tossed around over the centuries, their strengths and weaknesses, and how those strengths and weaknesses stack up against one another. Maybe, in your studies, you'll decide one standard is better than another, or maybe you'll remain skeptical that any standard can be justified reasonably. Maybe you'll come to believe that a person's actions can't be separated from their motives, and maybe you'll realize that your own moral stances on the issues of great importance to you are very difficult indeed to justify. If you don't take a class in ethics, and instead want to read in greater detail about these ideas that what I have presented here, you can begin by looking in the Appendix of this book for my suggestions for further reading. I'm sure you'll be amazed at just how far reaching and profound this topic really extends.

Chapter Two:
Thinking Critically about Abortion

There is hardly an issue one can think of that is more complicated, more troublesome, and more socially divisive than abortion. It is an issue that people feel so strongly about and so certain of, that they typically identify themselves with their position on it, and are often filled with intolerance and vitriol when they are confronted with opposing perspectives. Politically, abortion is a "litmus test" issue, separating one political camp from another. It is one of those issues that it is hardest to think critically about, because we feel so deeply the way we do about it. To question our position requires us to question ourselves, and our moral certainty, which is an uncomfortable intellectual task, leading most of us to not question our position on abortion at all.

But while it is okay to feel strongly about an issue, as I have repeatedly said throughout this book, we should also try and understand the support that our strong feelings rest upon. Also, since others feel strongly too, and yet have different positions, we should wonder how their strong feelings are supported, and try to understand how our own support stacks up against theirs. This is especially true of the issue of abortion, which brings to bear significant moral, religious, political, and social questions.

* * *

Is abortion murder? Is it, on the other hand, the unfettered constitutional right of every American woman, and the right of every woman, period, regardless of her national origin? Should it be regulated by the government in some way or should it be banned altogether? Is abortion more than just a "woman's issue", or should it be thought of as an important *human* issue? What has the United States Supreme Court said on these matters? In cases it has deliberated upon in the past, such as *Roe v. Wade*, what were the issues it heard from the opposing sides, and what were its rulings regarding those positions? How can these rulings help us to understand this issue, and how does the recent case of *Gonzales v. Carhart* change the landscape of how we understand the legal question of abortion? Do states have a stake in the life of an unborn child, and should that interest be taken into consideration when weighing the question of the legality of abortion? What about men? Do potential fathers have a stake, and should their feelings be accounted for in any law regarding the legality of

The Philosophy of Anything

abortion? When does life begin, and does it matter? Is an unborn baby like property, "belonging" to whomever is pregnant with it? Is it just a part of a pregnant person's body? Is it on the other hand an independent person, with rights and sovereignty, from the moment it is conceived? How do we frame the issue of abortion, and depending upon how we frame it, will that matter as to what kinds of questions we are able to answer, and our conclusions about each?

In this chapter, as in the last, I will present responses that address only a few of these many relevant questions, because to address them all is far beyond both the scope of my intentions, and I think the scope of possibility. Also as in the last chapter, in what follows I will not provide any definitive answers to the question of abortion, although my own perspective on this controversial issue will surely come out over the course of this chapter. But again, hopefully I will present a basis for your own investigation, and at least a beginning for you to better understand the varied and subtle problems that this issue represents, even perhaps in the face of your own position, and your certainty regarding it.

* * *

Virtually everyone is familiar with the labels that surround the issue of abortion in the manifestation of its public debate. Someone who is "pro-choice" is someone who believes that the decision to have an abortion should be up to the person who is pregnant, without the constraint of the government or of anyone else besides the pregnant person's physician. Someone who is "pro-life", by contrast, is someone who prioritizes the life of the unborn child over the choice of the mother.

But even characterizing these positions presents a dilemma that we must be aware of when we investigate the issue of abortion. How can we use neutral language that does not set the stage for conclusions, but merely presents the issue at hand? Does framing each position in terms of "prioritization", as I have done above really strike at the core of what is at stake, and does it do so neutrally? We surely cannot say, for instance, that by definition "abortion" is murder, and that pro-choice advocates are "baby-killers", since abortion being murder is the very claim that some people contentiously wish to make, and so should be argued for, and not simply stated from the out set as a given; also, to call pro-choice advocates baby killers is to malign the other side before debate even begins, and this is the antithesis of charitable inquiry. Similarly, it would be fallacious to say from the outset that restricting abortion is unconstitutional, since this is the very legal issue at hand when the Supreme Court deliberates on state statutes that attempt to restrict a woman's "right" to choose. If someone thinks proscribing abortion is unconstitutional, then the reasons that support this claim must be argued for. Notice too, even calling abortion a "right" is controversial. Some deny that it is, therefore, we cannot just assume it to be the case, without any further comment.

Furthermore, as seen above, in the rhetoric of each position, the opposing side is sometimes negatively characterized in such a way that before dialogue begins, the contrary

The Philosophy of Anything

perspective is vilified. For example, people who identify themselves as "pro-choice" might call pro-life supporters "anti-choice", while self-identified "pro-life" supporters call those who are pro-choice "anti-life", and as we saw above, "baby-killers". What is often implied, even if these explicitly acrimonious labels aren't used, is that someone who is an advocate for reproductive choice is an enemy of unborn life, and someone who is an advocate for unborn life is an enemy of reproductive choice. As with so many controversial issues, it seems that here there is an implicit fallacy committed before debate is even engaged; what in critical thinking parlance is called the "false dichotomy", or the idea that abortion is an either/or issue; that you're either pro-choice, or pro-life, and there's no in between. This tendency to slant the opposing side into merely the antithesis of one's own position represents the kind of fallacious beginning to argumentation that makes any kind of reasonable dialectic all but impossible, so no wonder why very little headway is ever achieved in the attempt to better understand the diversity of perspectives on this, as with so many other issues. Name calling, as most of us were taught at an early age, will get us nowhere.

* * *

Having said all this, framing the issue of abortion is problematic, even when we are aware of how our language impacts the debate, and even when we refrain from name calling. For instance, is abortion more of a moral issue or a legal issue? But if it's a legal issue, it still must be a moral issue, as we reasoned in the last chapter. There must be some moral basis for why we would make abortion illegal, or why we would keep it (mostly) legal. On the other hand, is abortion more of a political issue or is it more of a personal issue? Does it's legality or illegality matter more to society or to individuals? Does the moral status of abortion turn on cultural standards, or can we appeal to universal standards that make it right or wrong? Is abortion somehow all four kinds of issues: legal, moral, political, and individual? In other words, is abortion so complicated, touching upon such a wide variety of aspects of our lives, that no perspective takes precedence, or does one particular context matter more than another? Even if we decide that one context is more important than another, however, or even if we think they are all equally instructive to frame the issue, these four contexts do not by themselves represent every possible context either, but some other contexts can be seen as being combinations of them, inclusive of some, exclusive of others.

What about the religious context, for instance? That perspective of framing the issue involves issues of morality, personality, politics, and even legality, in some sense. Different people commonly follow various religious doctrines concerning the issue of abortion. In other words, it is an issue concerning which a great many people follow the position of their church, or their spiritual leaders. People in religious authority tell others they should feel a certain way about abortion, according to the teachings of their religion, and so the people who are not in positions of religious authority are convinced by those teachings or at least by that authoritative interpretation of those teachings.

The Philosophy of Anything

But what reasons do religious leaders give for their religion's position on this issue? Surely there are reasons why religious authorities feel one way or another about abortion, but where does the reasoning of the authorities end, and dogmatic (which is to say critically unexamined) assumptions of the people who follow that authority begin?

It should already be quite apparent how complicated this issue is, before we even begin to discuss the substance of opposing claims, and the argumentative merits that they rest upon. Especially when we begin to bring religion into the picture, we are on some very controversial ground, and people's sentiments are bound to be rubbed in the wrong way, no matter what is said. I'm sure many people who are reading this chapter now find my musings on this topic infuriatingly biased to one degree or another, but I would venture to say that this has less to do with my own certainty over what I feel about this issue, and more to do with the fact that most of us have already made up our minds about how we feel regarding abortion, and that because we are so entrenched in our views, we find it difficult to tolerate opposing (or even challenging) perspectives.

* * *

Here is one very simple example of a give and take on the issue of abortion that we hear quite often. It is an argumentative dialectic, which is to say that reasons are given in support of each conclusion, and rejoinders are offered for counterarguments to those claims, based upon reasons of their own. This is just one way a debate on abortion might proceed:

Argument: Abortion should be against the law, because it is murder.

Abortion should be illegal because it is an act of murder. Murder is wrong and against the law; therefore, abortion is wrong, and should be against the law.

An unborn child is a living, independent person, who possesses all the rights thereof. When a woman chooses to have an abortion, she commits murder on her unborn child. She should therefore be punished according to the penalties for committing murder. Doctors who perform abortions are complicit in the act of murder on unborn children. They should therefore be held accountable for their aiding the murder of unborn babies.

In California, 'murder' is defined as "the unlawful killing of a human being, or a fetus, with malice aforethought" (California Penal Code Section 187). Under this definition, an act is murder as long as the killing of another person is committed with malice aforethought. In other words, if someone kills someone else, and does so with the intent to kill, exhibiting a disregard for human life, then they commit murder. All abortions are committed with malice aforethought, in other words, abortions are by definition the killing of a person with intent to kill and a disregard for human life; therefore abortion rightly fits

42   *The Philosophy of Anything*

the definition of murder in the California Penal Code. Therefore a woman who chooses an abortion commits murder.

Counterargument to 'Abortion is murder'

If abortion were murder, then it should be against the law. But abortion is not an act of murder, therefore it is not a good reason to make it against the law. Although murder is wrong and against the law, since abortion is not murder, it should therefore not be against the law for that reason. Abortion, since it is not murder, should be legal.

When a woman receives an abortion, she does not commit murder on her unborn child; therefore, she should not be punished according to the penalties for committing murder. Doctors who perform abortions are therefore not complicit in acts of murder, and should therefore not be held accountable for their aiding the so-called murder of unborn children.

In California, although Section 187 of the Penal Code specifies 'murder' as being "the unlawful killing of . . . a fetus, with malice aforethought" (ibid.), there are exceptions to that definition, so that abortion is not considered murder if it is "solicited, aided, abetted, or consented to by the mother of the fetus" (ibid. Section 187.b.3). In other words, the California Penal Code defines murder so as to preserve the right of mothers to choose abortion. Also, to say that all abortions are committed with malice aforethought is a gross exaggeration. That is why the provisions of Section 187 of the California Penal Code specify exceptions to the definition of murder when concerning the termination of a fetus. For example, if a pregnant woman is killed maliciously, and her unborn child dies, then the killer can be charged with a double murder. But abortion is strictly ruled out of section 187, that is why the language "unlawful killing . . . of a fetus" is included, and not simply the word "abortion". Finally, to claim that all woman who choose an abortion have a disregard for human life is a hasty generalization. While some women might have repeated abortions, and feel no remorse for their actions, many women who choose abortion feel terrible about their choice, because of their strong feelings towards the life of their unborn child. Many women who choose abortion value life tremendously, so their choice to have an abortion is not chosen with malice aforethought.

Rejoinder to the Counterargument to 'Abortion is murder'

First, if it is granted that abortion is not an act of murder (that abortion is not committed with aforethought malice), this does not mean that abortion is therefore permissible and should remain legal. Other actions that involve the taking of human life are wrong and illegal, and fall short of murder; therefore, abortion can still be wrong and should still be illegal, even if it is not an act of murder.

Second, it is not at all clear according to the counterargument above that abortion is not an act of murder.

True, section 187 tries to distinguish abortion from the unlawful killing of a fetus, but this is just what is at stake in this debate. Abortion *should be considered to be the unlawful killing of a fetus*, since it is always performed with the intent to kill the fetus, and since to kill a fetus is malicious. Furthermore, there seems to be a double standard if we claim that when someone who is not the mother kills a fetus with malice aforethought they commit murder, while as long as a mother consents to killing the fetus it is somehow a legal abortion. Why should a mother's consent to kill a fetus be any different from someone else's killing of a fetus? Doesn't she intend to kill? Isn't the choice to have an abortion done with malice aforethought? But again, if we concede this point, we might still argue the slightly modified stance that:

Abortion is manslaughter

'Manslaughter' is defined in the California Penal Code, Section 192, as "the unlawful killing of a human being without malice". An unborn fetus is a human being. Granting that abortion is not murder, we may conclude that abortion is the unlawful killing of an unborn fetus without malice; therefore, abortion is manslaughter, and those committing abortion should be held accountable for the penalties of manslaughter. Furthermore, doctors who perform abortions are complicit in acts of manslaughter, and so should also be held accountable for that act.

Counter argument to "Abortion is Manslaughter"

If abortion is not murder, then abortion is not manslaughter either. Just because abortion is the killing of a fetus, it is not the *unlawful* killing of a fetus, period. If the drafters of the California Penal Code wished to define abortion as the unlawful killing of a fetus in any circumstance, then they would have done so. In other words, they would have made abortion illegal. But they did not. The purpose of section 192 of the California Penal Code, in contrast to the purpose of section 187, is to distinguish between the difference of unlawfully killing someone with malice aforethought versus killing someone without malice aforethought, be it a fetus or otherwise.

If someone wishes to claim that abortion should be considered the *unlawful* killing of a fetus, whether with malice aforethought or otherwise, this is something that needs to be argued for explicitly with reasons that support the conclusion. In other words, someone would need to provide reasons that support the conclusion that abortion should be considered unlawful. But using laws that are already on the books proscribing abortion as a reason to support the conclusion that abortion should be illegal, is not a good reason at all, especially when those laws on the books don't actually proscribe abortion. It merely begs the question, by restating as a premise what the conclusion tries to prove.

Furthermore, if a convincing argument is established that concludes that abortion should be considered a unlawful act, then it is incumbent upon Legislatures to write laws that express that

The Philosophy of Anything

explicitly. But when legislators have done so, they have usually not appealed to other laws so much as they have appealed to moral standards that for the most part sees *any* termination of a pregnancy as being morally reprehensible. An exception to this would be the recent Supreme Court decision of *Gonzales v. Carhart*, which saw a Federal law proscribing a *certain type* of abortion procedure upheld. Rather than proscribing abortion *per se*, the federal law proscribed a controversial way of performing an abortion. More on this case in just a moment, but note that appeal to laws in order to claim what one feels *should be* unlawful, but is not, is not a convincing way to argue for or against a claim.

* * *

As I alluded to above, abortion in the United States is, for the most part, legal. Already you should be scratching your head. "Wait a minute," I hope most people are asking themselves, "what about *Roe. Vs. Wade*? Didn't that Supreme Court decision make abortion totally legal? If so, how can abortion be 'for the most part' legal? That doesn't make sense." The short answer is that abortion is *not* totally legal, if by 'totally legal' one means 'unable to be constitutionally proscribed by law'.

First of all, there is no law that explicitly guarantees a woman's right to choose an abortion. But there are laws that try to limit a woman's choice. Secondly, Supreme Court decisions are *not* laws; they are decisions *about* laws. Effectively, the Supreme Court tells Legislative bodies that the laws they write either conform and adhere to the Constitution of the United

States, and so are legal, or that they do not, and so are illegal. State Legislative bodies and the Federal Legislature write and enact laws, and when those laws are violated and enforced, and then brought to trial, the judiciary decides if the law was violated, and eventually, if the law is Constitutionally sound. Sometimes judicial decisions are appealed, but the possibility of appealing a decision ends when a case is decided by the Supreme Court. The Supreme Court then has the final say as to whether a law is constitutional.

In *Roe vs. Wade*, perhaps the most important Judicial decision on the explicit question of abortion (and certainly the most popularly known decision on abortion), a Texas Law that proscribed abortions was contested, and the Supreme Court found that the Texas law violated the Constitution. Why? The reasons are complicated, but for one, the law was found not to give enough exception for the life and health of the mother; for another, the law was found to violate the "penumbral" right to privacy; finally, the law was found to violate the "due process" clause of the fourteenth amendment. But while *Roe vs. Wade* is the most popularly known abortion decision by the Supreme Court, it is far from being well understood by those who have heard of it. The truth of this statement is evinced if one simply reads the text of the majority opinion that called the Texas law proscribing abortion unconstitutional. It is filled with controversial material regarding for instance the penumbral "right to privacy", and the equally controversial "trimester rule", but one thing is plain: it does *not* establish a sweeping precedence of the illegality of legislation proscribing abortions, but instead, calls the Texas law

The Philosophy of Anything

under its consideration illegal, and leaves the door open for future legislation that proscribes abortion according to certain guidelines. In other words, *Roe v. Wade* is not the rock solid judicial decision guaranteeing a woman's right to choose that many people think of it as being. This is pivotal to understanding the abortion debate, at least in a legal and political sense, because it flies in the face of the common understanding of *Roe v. Wade*, namely, that the decision unequivocally establishes a woman's right to choose.

State legislators across the country who believe that abortion is immoral and should be illegal (and who presumably represent voters who believe these things as well) continue to write legislation that attempts to find the Constitutional soundness that no abortion legislation has yet been able to achieve. No abortion legislation, that is, until the Federal legislation proscribing a certain abortion procedure that was challenged in the case of *Gonzales v. Carhart*. Interestingly, the decision of *Gonzales v. Carhart* upheld the Federal law proscribing an abortion procedure that *does not* make exceptions for the life and health of the mother. This flies in the face of precedent decisions on abortion, which have left room for legislation proscribing abortion as long as it makes those exceptions. This is a pivotal moment in judicial precedent for this issue, because it redefines what is acceptable abortion legislation.

* * *

But to proceed: legally, the issue of abortion arises because some people take a moral stance of opposition, and then try to make that moral stance law. Since they are against abortion, and see it as a moral issue, they then try and make abortion illegal. Still, legally the issue comes up as well because people are unwilling to have the government regulate the medical choices they make with their doctors regarding their health, and so abortion regulations are challenged in the courts. It is here that the moral conviction of some people begins to affect the practical lives of others in a very real way. But the same can be said of those who take a moral stance in favor of abortion. Since they tend to feel that a woman's right to choose abortion for herself is a moral issue, they want to interpret the law in such a way as to protect that right from any kind of legal or governmental infringement. So morality tends to translate into legality; or to put it a bit differently, morality inspires legality. But again, what is legal is not necessarily moral. In our attempt to justify why abortion should remain legal, for instance, we cannot appeal to the mere fact that it is at this point in time legal. We need *reasons* why it should be so, that go beyond the legal issues, and point to some sort of justification for the issue itself. We do this by appealing to values that we think range over the issue at hand.

The issues surrounding abortion, however, at least as it is debated in the public sphere, among voters who are for the most part ignorant regarding the legal distinctions and issues, concern personal feelings that are seldom questioned, because they are so difficult to provide reasons for that are not wholly subjective. For instance, as we have seen, those who seek to proscribe abortion

The Philosophy of Anything

often claim that it is murder, at whatever stage of the pregnancy. This is based upon the assumption that life begins at conception, and that a conceived human should be afforded all the rights of a developed person. This attitude comes from, among other things, a religious doctrine that emphasizes the sanctity of unborn life. But the abortion debate as it is framed by the Supreme Court has very little to do with the existential or personal or political status of a fetus. In fact, it instead has almost everything to do with the rights of the pregnant woman, who carries that fetus as a part of her own body.

But even our terminology is confusing, and those immersed within the debate may take exception to my characterization of it, for other reasons too, perhaps, but if only because of the ambiguous and contentious language I am using to describe the problem. When a sperm fertilizes a human egg, is the zygote a living human? Is it wrong to call it a fetus? Is it more appropriate to call it an unborn baby? Does it matter where in the development of the embryo we define it's personhood to begin? Some people are opposed to embryonic stem cell research, because it destroys a cell that could potentially become human. If even cells that are not developing human fetuses deserve rights, what does that say about a fertilized egg? These are the kinds of questions that need to be examined when you investigate your own position on abortion. None have easy answers, and all are contentious. But they offer a way to begin to think about the problem in a constructive and critical way, that's gets down to the underpinnings of our positions. If you can reason out these questions, and try and understand how they bear on the problem itself, you'll be in a much better position to justify how you feel about abortion.

* * *

When I think about abortion, whether it is right or wrong, or just what the issue involves, I find myself attempting to find and justify a mediated stance that tries to accept the spirit of the perspectives from both extremes, while refraining from accepting fully their opposing conclusions. However, on its face, many would see this sort of position, without knowing the details of it, as being mediated in the worst possible way. Or, to put it differently, many people feel that any mediated stance on abortion is just capitulation in the face of an issue that deserves an uncompromising position, for or against. Again, there are some who strenuously believe that abortion is in fact murder, at any time after conception, and that there are no exceptions to this rule. Life begins at conception, and if you end that life, you commit murder, period. There are also those who believe, just as uncompromisingly, that a woman has a right to an abortion with no exception, and that, especially in the early stages of pregnancy, the developing fetus is not yet a person. For these people, abortion is permissible, always. In either case, though, many people are convinced that abortion is either/or, black or white issue, and any middle ground is impossible. Those who do take the middle ground, according to many, are somehow missing the point.

The Philosophy of Anything

Let me illustrate some extremely held dogmatic positions concerning the rightness or wrongness of abortion. When, for instance, a 13-year-old girl is raped and impregnated by her stepfather, and then chooses to have an abortion, or when a woman will die if she brings her pregnancy to term, and so too chooses to have an abortion, or when a woman takes a morning after pill in order to not become pregnant, then a stringent pro-life advocate might say that those who make these choices, though they are committing no crime that is on the books, nevertheless commit murder, and so should not be legally allowed to do so. Abortion is abortion, detractors of the procedure say, and should be proscribed, whether a woman chooses to have one as a result of rape or incest, months after conception, or whether she chooses to have one because to carry her pregnancy to term would mean her death or her failure of health. Detractors of abortion say that abortion is abortion, even in the case of the morning after pill, when a fertilized egg is expelled only hours or days after the zygote is formed, and a woman's "pregnancy" is merely a lump of dividing cells that has not yet become attached to the uterine wall. (Note the quotations: The word "pregnant" itself, however colloquially understood, is nevertheless a term whose definition is controversial. "When does pregnancy begin?" This question is central in the debate concerning abortion.)

Contrarily, from the extreme perspective of dogmatic pro-choice advocates, to prohibit a woman from having an abortion, even at the very end of her pregnancy, and even if the pregnant woman's life or health is not threatened by carrying her pregnancy to term, and even if labor has to be induced in order to terminate the pregnancy, is abhorrent to that woman's reproductive rights. For such pro-choice advocates, the state has no legitimate right to infringe upon a woman's right to choose an abortion under any circumstances, even if it means, for all practical purposes, in delivering a close to term, viable fetus in such a way as to end its life.

My own feelings about this issue might now start to become more apparent. The three examples I mentioned above concerning which pro-life advocates would argue that abortion should not be allowed are cases that I am inclined to believe that abortion should be allowed, because of interest of maintaining individual rights; and the case concerning which pro-choice advocates would argue that abortion should be allowed I am inclined to believe that abortion should not be allowed, because of the interest in preserving unborn life.

I feel I want to reject the position that states that abortion should be outlawed altogether, and regulated no matter what. In addition, I feel I want to reject the position that states that a woman has a right to choose an abortion, no matter what. Some people would therefore call me pro-choice, in no uncertain terms, since I do in fact believe that women have certain reproductive rights, and that one of those rights is to choose to have abortion. But on the other hand, pro-choice advocates would have a problem with my position, and might call me, if not pro-life, at least anti-choice, since I think that a pregnant woman does not, in all instances, have an *unfettered* right to choose to have an abortion. And I think both camps are somehow right about my position: I am in some ways pro-choice, and I am in some ways pro-life. But I also think that both camps are somehow wrong: labels can be misleading, and only speak of generalities that do not touch upon the very complicated and subtle problems that an issue like abortion raises. I am neither pro-choice nor pro-life, but attempt to formulate a position on a subject that admits of complex subtleties that genuinely baffle me at times, and that are difficult to come to terms with. In a situation like this, the labels we use to categorize ourselves and others become unhelpful, and do more harm than good.

You should be asking: How can someone accept abortion on one hand, and reject it on the other? Here is where the debate can be engaged, here is the possibility of shared understanding, even if it ends in disagreement. In each case, through critical inquiry, I reject the extreme positions that allow no shade of gray. But in each case, from the perspective of the supporters of either extreme, I unconscionably yield ground when I should be uncompromising. How to reason out my position? How to back it up? I think the answer, at least as a beginning, is to do what I am doing now: To freely explore the different avenues that need further attention and careful inquiry. To discover the questions that I must attend to in order to better understand this issue.

But this chapter is not supposed to be about my position. I include a watered down expression of it here to suggest how the topic might proceed, and again, to spark meaningful thought about this most important subject.

* * *

When I think about the issue of abortion, I think about the people who make the choice, and their unborn children. I think of all the varied cases and circumstances that surround that choice and those people. I think of what happens when medically safe abortions are not available, and women try to give themselves abortions. I think of close-to-term unborn babies that are so near their lives outside of the womb that to call them people is intuitive and unavoidable. I think of how difficult the decision to choose an abortion must be for those women who are faced with the choice, and I am struck dumb, filled with compassion for their situation.

And I'd like to end this chapter on that note. We cannot forget that abortion is complicated, and that it involves real choices and real people making those choices, with all their complicated thoughts and feelings and circumstances. I think if we have learned anything from this discussion, it should be that there are so many facets to the issue, and so many ways of approaching it, that blanket statements regarding it almost invariably fail to do justice to the nuances of what is involved when a woman chooses to have an abortion. If we are to critically and constructively think about this issue, then we need to do it calmly, and logically, knowing that disagreement is inevitable, but recognizing that those who disagree with us might have something to offer in the reasons they have that support their views, and acknowledging that the other side are not villains.

When we think about abortion, then, we need to do so charitably. That is to say, we need to try and withhold final judgment until all the reasoning is out on the table. Part of this is

The Philosophy of Anything

to recognize that there might not even be such a thing as a final judgment. And even if there is a sense of finality in your certainty, we need to examine that reasoning that supports it with an open mind, and we need to confront other perspectives with the same openness, and not condemn a perspective outright, even if we feel certain that it is wrong. We do well to remember that the common bond we share in our grappling with this issue is that we all understand that life and liberty is precious. How to preserve that strong intuition in the face of such a complicated and controversial issue like abortion, maintaining a level of respect for people with contrary views, and all the while genuinely seeking an increased understanding of what is at stake, is the greatest challenge when we try to think critically about this issue.

Chapter Three:

Thinking Critically about War

Although I am repulsed by the realities of war, I still really enjoy war movies. The fascinating stories of survival and brutality, of glory and defeat, of heroism and humiliation, astound me. I find myself enthralled by the depictions of brotherhood and survival and honor, ironically coupled with hostility and death and shame. There's something amazing about how the images are reflections of reality, how the narratives are stories that have been lived, and yet how, regardless of their historical reference, the films are nevertheless renderings, and fictions. However many war films I watch, there's something humbling about how I'm never any closer to truly understanding what war is about, for those who have to fight it and live it.

Then there's the awareness of war that I have in addition to the veneer of understanding that comes from whatever war movies I might watch. There's the understanding that comes from my personal experience as a young American, a person whose recent generations of family members have been there, in combat: in the Pacific and in Europe during World War II, and in Vietnam, Bosnia, and the Gulf more recently. There's the perspective I have as a college instructor, who saw one of his students deployed to Iraq in mid-semester, and whose same student submitted his final paper from a combat zone. This kind of experience inspires in me a feeling of solidarity with my compatriots, uniting me with the men and women my own age and younger, who are right now risking and giving their lives in an effort to fight for our country, and for other, even more uncertain things. There's also the daily reminder from the news, that in addition to those who die in combat, in uniform, the casualties of war tragically affect most of all the innocents who are caught in the middle: the citizens who do not fight, but who experience war on their doorstep, on their soil, and in their everyday lives. There's the knowledge from this that however far removed from the battlefield I might personally be, the battlefield itself is potentially not so far away. And finally, there is the awesome stillness and silent respect that overcomes me when I see, flashed on the news in a momentary memorial, as their deaths are made official and their photographs become available, the names and faces of service personnel killed in Iraq and Afghanistan. When I see those faces and read those names, I know that war is real, is really happening, is really saving and destroying lives, and is really a part of the world.

War films remind me of what I know about war apart from the fictional stories, apart from the renderings, and bring these thoughts home to me; they remind me of the reality of war, and they reinforce the conviction that however gruesome and frightening war is, and however painful a subject it might be, it is still worth thinking about, and perhaps especially because of its gruesomeness and horror, still worth questioning.

* * *

Is war natural? Is it a part of human nature? Is violence in general something innate, a part of us we can never be rid of? If war is not biologically inevitable, it is nevertheless socially necessary? Must we fight in order to survive as a nation, a country, a culture? When is war justified, if it is ever justified at all, and when is it not? Will there ever be peace, or is peace impossible because of the kind of being that human beings are? These questions and many others have been pondered for a very long time indeed, but it seems we are no closer to answers that are immune to criticism as we are to answering questions of human nature more grandly, or any philosophical or deep and timeless human question, like whether God exists, or what makes something right, or when personhood begins, or how we can know anything at all.

What is war, anyway? Do we even have a grasp of what the word means? When one seeks to understand the meaning of a word, looking up definitions in the dictionary is a good place to begin, but almost never a good place to end. This is especially true if we're trying to critically examine a concept, and not just understand how people sometimes employ it. In other words, dictionaries can reliably tell us how a word is commonly used in its various senses, but if we wish to deeply examine a word, an idea, perhaps the common usages will not exhaustively explain what it means conceptually, in all its various manifestations and implications. This is certainly true of the word "war". Such a complicated idea cannot be elucidated just by seeing how we use it, although an examination of its use might help to tease out its meaning.

Up until now, we have had many occasions in this book where we could have turned to the dictionary in order to elucidate meaning, and clarify concepts. For instance, maybe we could have looked up the words "pregnancy" and "murder", in the last chapter on abortion to see what ideas those words usually describe; maybe we could have looked up the words "moral" and "ethical" in the chapter on our moral certainty to see if there was any difference between the two. But while definitions, if we can agree upon them, offer a certain amount of control and consistency to our inquiries, they do not solve those inquiries themselves. While they might help to make our critical investigations more precise, they do not answer those critical investigations finally.

There is one dictionary, though, that gives us a great deal of insight into words, both their history and their meaning. The Oxford English Dictionary (Oxford University Press, ©1971) has this (among other things) to say of the word *war*:

It is a curious fact that no Germanic nation in early historic times had in living use any word properly meaning 'war', though several words with that meaning survived in poetry, in proverbial phrases, and in compound personal names. The Romanic-speaking peoples, who were obliged to avoid the L. *bellum* on account of its formal coincidence with *bello-* beautiful, found no nearer equivalent in Teut. than *werra*.

Curious indeed. How remarkable that the ancient Germanic peoples, who have a long history of violent conflict, didn't have a word for war, except poetically? Surely the history of this word in English cannot result from the Germanic tribes never experiencing war, for history speaks overwhelmingly to the contrary. And how fascinating it is that the word for "war" in Latin so closely resembles the word for "beautiful", even if only coincidentally! Is it possible that the Romans regarded their way of waging war as a sort of art form? Surely the irony of the resemblance of these Latin words has some significance to our own use of the word "war"? Don't we ourselves view war as a sort of art?

At some point, though, like all words, the word "war" came to be used to describe something about human experience that needed a name. So war has been around for a long time, and longer, presumably, then when there was even a word for it. And this artificiality that comes along with the definition of the word and the word itself should be examined when we think of what war means, not just as we conceptualize it, but as it is experienced. That is to say, might war as it is *practiced* and understood by humans, be *invented* by us too? Is war something that is not natural at all?

In the first half of this chapter, I will briefly explore war as being a natural versus an artificial human endeavor. I think the most poignant question we can ask about war is to inquire as to its cause: whether organized violence is a biological necessity, a part of human nature that we can do nothing to stop, or whether it is not, but something we create ourselves, consciously. Furthermore, we should ask whether war is somehow both. As in the previous chapters, I do not pretend to answer this daunting question, although I do hope to make the reader better aware of it.

In the second half of this chapter I will then briefly address what I see as a particularly infamous example of war, as it is being practiced right now by the United States, in what has become a very troubling state of current world affairs. The reason why I think talking about war *in theory* is so significant is that, as we speak, we are *in practice* embroiled in a divisive and devastating war. When we talk about war, then, we must remind ourselves that we are presently not removed from its problematic reality.

Now, will this second discussion be dated? Yes. It involves an examination of current events that will obviously remain current only for a brief time. Some people will object that to include such a discussion weakens the presentation of the issue, because it anchors us too firmly in what will soon be history. But I think the events that will soon be history are what make the topic of war in general so relevant right now. Will it be considered polemic? Probably, since the disinterested perspective one gains from hindsight is mostly absent in the midst of controversial politics and policy that are currently unfolding. Some people will object that this takes away the objectivity of the

The Philosophy of Anything

discussion, because it is so obviously biased. But I also see this as being beneficial to the goal of illustrating the idea that the topics we think about must be things we care and feel deeply about; and in any case, as I said in the Preface, I am not trying to be objective. Will it be helpful for those who read it in their effort to think critically about this controversial issue? I hope so, if it does so only by reminding us of the extraordinary events that are transpiring abroad as we continue to live our ordinary lives at home. Some people will think that this discussion is unhelpful, since it occurs in the voice of heated passion as opposed to the voice of cold logic. But I believe this chapter succeeds, if it only manages to present a spirited challenge for those with opposing perspectives to rebut, and for those of like-minded perspectives to support. Some people might complain that in the second part of this chapter I speak less about *how to* think about war and merely present *what I* think about war. This is not altogether a false characterization. But I encourage readers to view my personal perspective with a critical eye, and to think about the issue of war in general from the perspective of the issue of war in particular. Having said this, I will now proceed.

* * *

What are the common usages of the word *war*? Well, of course, it depends upon what dictionary one uses, but one way we might begin examining the concept is the everyday way people use the word that describes it. First, we should acknowledge how it is used in its metaphorical sense: When people have a "war of words", or when two neighbors are "at war" over the issue of who stole who's cat, to take a random example, it makes sense to use this word. And who could forget Nancy Reagan's "war on drugs", just to give another example? When we use the word "war" metaphorically, we are talking about a state of hostile affairs. We are talking about contention and conflict, between people with uncompromising positions that are in opposition to one another.

This of course is what constitutes the basis of the word "war" when we use it in a literal sense too, although there is one major difference. War, literally, is when sovereign states, or nations, or geographies, or peoples, or cultures, are in hostile opposition to one another, and mobilize into groups of themselves to engage in violence, and the killing of members of the opposing group or groups, to effect some goal. War in its literal sense is about violence, hostility, and organized killing, usually orchestrated by leaders, usually to effect some kind of self-interested purpose for the state, the culture, the group, or the leaders themselves.

This, to foreshadow a future discussion, is why it makes a certain amount of sense to say that the United States is engaged in a "war on terror". Our government is engaged in a violent conflict with an enemy group: terrorists. But what makes the war on terror different is that "terror" is an idea, or really, an emotion. Are we at war with an idea, an emotion, or with people who subscribe to the idea, and inspire the emotion? Maybe both. Al-Qaeda is our enemy, obviously, but why not then say that we are at war with Al-Qaeda? It seems clear that the reason is that, first,

The Philosophy of Anything

Al-Qaeda is a terrorist organization that is not a sovereign state, so to declare war on Al-Qaeda is problematic; second, that Al-Qaeda is not the only group that wishes us harm, so the war we wage against Al-Qaeda is only part of the war we are fighting; and third, that Al-Qaeda as an organization represents an idea or a mentality, namely, an ideology of terrorism, that somehow transcends the group itself. Still, if the war on terror is really an apt name for the conflict we are engaged in, one wonders how this war will ever end, since victory usually happens when a government surrenders, and since because there is no government we are fighting, there can be no surrender. It follows that as long as there is one terrorist who is willing to do the United States harm, whether they are a part of Al-Qaeda or not, the war on terror will continue. This is surely unlike war as we typically understand it. But leaving aside until later a discussion of the current war, and the war on terrorism, let us return to a discussion concerning war in general.

Once we feel that we have a handle on what war means, one question that should also not be answered too quickly, and that might not be able to be answered at all, is: "what is the cause of war?" Why would we ask this question? Obviously it has some practical significance, but I think most significantly, we can ask this question in order perhaps to illuminate an answer to another question, which is "how can war be prevented?"

Back to the idea of war as a natural tendency. This is one quick answer some might give when trying to discover the cause of war (and not of particular wars, but of war as a human activity). Is war inevitable? Is violence and killing a part of human nature? These are questions that are perhaps unanswerable in any kind of final sense; they are true philosophical questions in that our reason points to different, justifiable answers, and no amount of empirical evidence (it seems) will solve the problem for us. Dictionaries might give a general idea of what war is, but there is no book that can ultimately answer the question of why war exists. We need a science of war, in other words, a way of figuring out why war is the way it is, and why there is war at all. But is any expectation that we can "discover" the cause of war like we hope to "discover" the cause of cancer, a naive attempt at something beyond our grasp? Maybe. It still makes sense, though, to investigate this question. I think we should still try to understand what about ourselves leads to this aspect of our behavior that is so frightening, and that so many of us take as a matter of course.

Again, war can be construed as meaning any state of affairs whereby there is strife and struggle, hostility and violent conflict. Usually war also involves politics, which is to say governments and the people who control them, acting in some sort of self-interested way. Although not all wars are fought for self-interested objectives, the self-interest that is seen in many conflicts can be varied: to procure economic or geographical gain for the country as a whole or for elements within a country; to maintain security and fight for national survival as a defensive tactic in the face of aggression; to do battle against differing ideologies that threaten a way of life. However diverse the self-interested motives are for war, though, the violent conflicts between nations are carried out by many people, but decided to be engaged in by few.

This leads us to the relationship between politics and war. Perhaps war has always involved politics of more or less one sophisticated sort or another. Because it seems that war is something that is decided upon; in other words, it does not just happen of its own accord, spontaneously. Even militias have leaders, and though they might not be affiliated with any government, they still have control over those under them. People must decide to engage in war, and usually the people who decide are people who wield a great amount of political power. So whether it is a matter of aggression or not, self-interest in one form or another or not, war, in almost all its instances, is the outcome of decision makers in positions of power. Violence might be perpetrated by individuals, but war is an organized and orchestrated endeavor that individuals not in positions of power do not usually make on their own. If this is true, and war is something is decided upon by individuals making those decisions in the name of large groups of others, how can we say it is an instinctual behavior? How can we say war is natural if it is something that happens between societies, and that the leaders of those societies decide upon?

War is so deeply rooted in human custom, it is almost impossible to know how to begin to determine its origin or cause or source in our complicated history as a species. Indeed, can such things even be determined? Some claim it is not merely a matter of human custom, but of human *nature*, and the truthfulness of this claim has been debated at length in contemporary literature and throughout intellectual history. War is sometimes seen as a sort of Darwinian outcome of scarcity, a competition for limited natural resources, and a fight for survival. In this sense war is interpreted as a more complicated aspect of what all life is programmed to do: live and thrive as best it can.

But at the very least war is also a part of human custom, and one is tempted to say human habit. Perhaps it *is* in our genes, whatever that means, but it is very much so in our history, and our society, and our lives, and it is hard to imagine a time without it. Then again, it is hard to imagine a time without language, or society, and we suspect there was such a time in human history too, so why should a time before war be so hard to imagine?

On the other hand, war *is* a human activity, to the extent that *our* kind of war seems not so much to be a behavior deriving from nature, as the biological explanation would have it, but rather from our own peculiarity as so-called rational animals. But is this just what is meant when people say that war is natural? Is it just another way of resting the explanation on our biology? After all, our rationality is surely a matter of our biology, is it not? Does this perspective then just mean that humans, being humans, must inevitably make war? Indeed, it is hard to see how there is anything *but* "our kind" of war, since to ascribe war to animals does not make intuitive sense, and on the face of it seems to be the most abject sort of anthropomorphism. But this is not to say that we do not do this. How frequently do we label competition in nature not as the playing out of inevitable and unaware behaviors, and instead see our own tendencies in reflection, when we notice the conflicts between lions and hyenas, for instance, or between any number of species in geographies where water is scarce, and "hostilities" ensue? When we look at other primates, for example, what do we see in their inter- and intra- species conflicts but a sort of mirroring of the conflicts we ourselves are so familiar with?

Yet this seems wrong. Is war really something that animals engage in? Do they really organize themselves in the same way that we do, in order to kill, in order to conquer? If they do not, is the behavior at least analogous? Perhaps. But the aptness of the analogy fails when we consider the very complicated conflicts that occur between people, when measured against the comparatively unconscious and instinctual activity of animals. And humans are certainly animals, no doubt about it, and are instinctual creatures, but aren't we somehow special, and doesn't war seem to be part of the special brand of beings we are? If war is instinctual too, how does it (if it does at all) transcend that instinctual impetus of aggression and violence, and how can we explain the fact that we are able to control and resist that instinct as it manifests itself in organized societal ways, and avoid war even when we are tempted to engage in it?

How are we special? Well, language, of course, and reason, and our self-consciousness and the complicated emotions we can name, and the magnificent way our intelligence enables us to make and use tools unlike any other creature, manipulating our environment as we see fit. Now, tools are artificial, which is to say man-made, which is to say not natural. It is not an innate part of human nature that allows us to make tools, otherwise we would always have made them, and it seems that this is not the case. While humans themselves might be a part of nature, somehow the things that we are capable of are not natural, the things we do are artificial, made by man, separated from nature. Of course we are biological, but somehow we are more than our mere biology, somehow we have a free will (that some people deny this, of course, is not really the issue), somehow we make choices and do things of our volition, somehow we make conscious decisions, weighing alternatives, and use reason to decide. The human brain is the most complicated specimen, for although we are quite alike other animals in our chemical and genetic composition, we nevertheless think of ourselves as superior to and different from other forms of life, because of our intelligence, and I think rightly so. Why? Does our capacity for organized violence have anything to do with this?

Is war then really a human habit, no matter what else it is? Doesn't it make sense to think of war as another tool humans have devised? And has there ever really been peace? If there hasn't, does this help to support the claim that war is an innate part of human nature? It seems like peace is just the time in between the hostilities of war, and if this is true, and societies are always either at war or in between them, then what really is the value of peace, or is it just an illusion? Is our tendency to kill each other so ingrained or such a natural part of who we are that to not kill each other is unnatural?

And is it so unjustifiable to call war a societal habit? Perhaps an even stronger word is needed, and we should label war, not as our mere habit, but as humanity's most lethal *addiction*. In fact, it seems as though, since we are constantly engaging in it and defending its necessity, while (at least publicly) simultaneously repudiating and disparaging its cost in human life, we are caught in the classic circle of self-deception Alcoholics Anonymous members and other substance abusers call *denial*. Nowadays, of course, there is supposed to be a gene that signals a risk of having addictive personality traits, so maybe war does indeed have something to do with our genes, even if it is just another kind of self-destructive and generally malfeasant and inveterate human pathology. Perhaps there is a modicum of aptness in this analogy, and perhaps this analogy fails too, but since it is clear that war has been a human activity for so long, how else can we think of war other than it being a natural, or at least habitual endeavor?

But regardless as to whether we are genetically disposed to war, which to me seems somewhat unlikely, or if it is a self-destructive and artificial endeavor (although it is hard to see how either side could be proved), what is important to remember is that we kill things, we kill each other, and we kill each other in a terrifyingly organized manner. And even if there is some middle ground, and the issue is not black or white, either/or, and there is no excluded middle, on the whole it must be acknowledged that we do a whole lot of killing. Who is the "we"? People, societies, cultures. People, nations, governments. People, individuals, soldiers. Some individuals are opposed to the killing. Some find it distasteful, but necessary. Some exhilarate in it. There are those who will not eat meat because of the violence involved, and there are people who protest war; then there are those who think some wars make sense, and others do not. Still, all in all, we do a lot of killing, regardless of the diversity of perspectives. Regardless of how we feel about war, it continues to be waged.

Killing other humans is especially frightening today, too, because of the modern technology we have to accomplish it. It is not just how organized we can be in our effort to kill each other that is so astounding, but the methods we employ in that organization: Weapons of mass destruction, and nuclear weapons especially, are perhaps the most awe-inspiringly horrendous weapons that one can imagine. What makes them even more terrifying is that they are controlled by a handful of individual heads-of-state, any of whom, at their will, can push a button and bury humanity in a cloud of radioactive dust. How close were we to a nuclear holocaust, back in the early 1960's? How close did we come to the doomsday WWIII scenario many people (legitimately) fear? So close, says former Secretary of Defense Robert S. McNamara in the documentary film *The Fog of War* (2003), that Fidel Castro had already given the orders to launch against targets in the United States if President Kennedy had decided to invade Cuba in 1962. Furthermore, especially today, with the threat of terrorism, the proliferation of nuclear weapons represents perhaps the most troubling threat to the United States, and the world at large.

As the noted scientist and television producer James Burke said at a recent lecture series in Oakland regarding global warming: "Does it really matter how it came to be? Isn't it enough that it exists? Shouldn't we try and do something about it?" I believe the same can be said of war. Obviously, there are very interesting philosophical questions one can ask and try to answer

The Philosophy of Anything

in an effort to better understand war and its causes, but knowing that it exists is perhaps enough for us to debate less upon theoretical postulations, and more upon the reality of what we should do in a world where we are all affected by the actual consequences and potential catastrophes of war. If war is an artificial endeavor, then there is presumably a way to for humans to avoid it, and we need to think about this if we are to understand war and its very real and troubling effects.

* * *

This is especially true today, in the United States, where American citizens like myself are to one degree or another complicit in our military's protracted occupation of Iraq, whether we support the occupation or not. Currently, though, popular support for this "war" is the lowest it has ever been. The President's "policy" has been steadily waning, even (and most significantly) from within his own political party. In addition, recent polls show the majority of Americans believe the war was a mistake, even if the majority still believe that to withdraw "precipitously" from Iraq would also be a mistake, and even if many find it hard to see how a phased withdraw after four years of occupation could be considered precipitous to begin with.

Despite this lack of support, however, the protests and popular unrest that occurred before the war began and that furthermore occurred in past conflicts that were vastly unpopular is shamefully absent today, as the events in Iraq continue. While Iraqi civilians die every day by the dozens, while American and

Iraqi soldiers are unconventionally attacked by insurgent elements within a civil war, while the President's policy has continually failed to successfully adapt to the strategic changes in the theater, the American public is still passively standing by, as impotent and inept as the President seems to be, watching agape as this foreign policy blunder unfolds.

Let me illustrate: recently, on the San Francisco State University campus, in a rare show of solidarity, students staged a walk-out, leaving their classrooms to shout slogans and to protest something that hit them very close to home: Fee hikes for the next school year. Yes, it's true, students at SFSU were more motivated and unified to shout their protest about a few hundred dollars, than they were to shout about three thousand dead American soldiers; they were more likely to organize a protest because of their wallets, than they were because of their war.

Is it really "their" war, though? I have a feeling most students on the SFSU campus would disavow their ownership in this war if they were asked if it was theirs. Is it "our" war, then, even if we are opposed to it?

If it is, what can we point to that shows that Americans take ownership of it? Should we look at the magnetic yellow ribbons that some people slap on the trunks of their cars, as they fill up with gasoline that, despite the recent increase in refined oil prices nationwide, remains the cheapest in the world? Or does this speak to the contrary? Do we see it in a military that is struggling to meet its recruitment goals, and that lowers its standards for enlistment? Or does this speak to the contrary? Do we see it in the permanent income tax-cut that chokes our national

The Philosophy of Anything

revenue and spending power, or in the curious absence of war bonds, or in the unwillingness of citizens and our government to ration resources? Do we see it in the resolve of American citizens in the face of this conflict, telling our leaders that we are willing to fund this war with something other than deficit spending and debt, and that American soldiers and their families are not the only ones who are willing to sacrifice? Or do these things overwhelmingly speak to the contrary, and prove how little ownership the American public is willing to take for Iraq?

Democrats in Congress just recently acquiesced to an emergency spending bill for the war that sets no time limits for withdrawal (all previous attempts to tie such time-tables to funding being vetoed by the President), yet by the fall of 2007 our commanding General will report on the progress (or lack thereof) of the new "surge" policy in Baghdad, and it is unclear how a negative report will affect our troop deployment. It is unclear whether pressure from Congress will change the President's policy. It is unclear whether we will continue to fail in Iraq, not because of a lack of the bravery, skill, and dedication that most of us believe the American soldier possesses, but because of a civilian-side strategy and management that cannot cope with the unique challenges this war turned out to deliver.

But perhaps this surprises no one, since for the past four years Americans have been dying and progress has been unapparent, since war was never formally declared by Congress, and since a National election looms on the not too distant horizon, and the last election saw a change of power in the Congress. Perhaps we should expect the President, whose approval rating is the lowest it has ever been, in his last two years in office, to remain stubborn in the face of his failing policy, and to stay the course: his approval rating, like the security situation in Baghdad and across Iraq, sinking even lower. However, the President's approval rating is not necessarily a good measure of how the war is actually proceeding. It rather states something that is open to much less interpretation: that however incremental steps forward we might be making in Iraq, or however many backward steps we might be making, those steps are not enough for the explicit support of the majority of the American public.

* * *

Let's take a step back ourselves, and notice how, regardless of whether you take exception to these thoughts, in the beginning of the last section I put the words "war" and "policy" in quotes, in reference to the President's decisions regarding Iraq. Is the American occupation of Iraq a war? Doesn't *Congress* declare war, and if the President inherently has the right to use the military without congressional approval, doesn't he or she then need to at some point *get* that approval, in order for the war to continue to be prosecuted? But *did* the President get that approval? We often hear of the "Iraq War Resolution" passed by Congress in 2002. Yes, this gave the President the "authority" to enforce, as he saw fit, the resolutions passed by the United Nations, even if we saw the United Nations as itself not wishing to enforce those resolutions. Yes, it was passed in the aftermath of 9/11, when we rightly saw our national security as being at grave risk. But was the resolution, which was directed towards Saddam Hussein, his regime, *and* terrorism in general, equivalent to a declaration of war? The answer is not so clear, but it seems on the face of it that, since there is such a thing as an explicit declaration of war, and since such a declaration was *not* explicitly made by Congress (however implicitly they made such a declaration with the resolution), we may conclude that we are not *technically* at war, since war was not *formally* declared. This is not to say that it doesn't make sense to say that we are at war in Iraq, for we are certainly engaged in open hostilities with an enemy, but it is to say that if we are to be accurate, we need to separate the colloquial understanding of "war", which we see today in Iraq, with the more technical definition of war that sees Congress as having the ultimate authority in any long term engagement.

On the one hand, Congress' resolution was a "use of force" resolution, and certainly gave approval for the President to make the kinds of decisions that are inherently the President's to make anyway. In other words, Congress merely gave the President an official nod to do what he deemed necessary, with the knowledge that he could do so even without that nod of approval. On the other hand, though, the resolution was not a declaration of war, and the President, while acting with the approval of Congress in 2002, now has seen that Congressional support wane to the point that funding for the war has stalled, and is only grudgingly being provided without deadlines for withdraw. How much is Congress and the people that Congress represents in favor of the President's policy, now that it has proven to be so disastrous? How sanctioned is this war anyway? How can anyone reasonably convince us that it is *ours* when most of us do not trust the President, however well intentioned he might arguably be, to successfully achieve whatever it is we are supposed to be achieving over there? Even the goals of this war are ambiguous.

But it *is* our war. However much some of us might scream "not in my name", it is our war, because it is our country, our citizenship, or government that is prosecuting it. However much what we are trying to achieve in Iraq is unclear, *we* are still trying to achieve it. "We", meaning *our* treasure, *our* young people, *our* effort, even if the American public as a whole is dissatisfied, and unwilling to sacrifice. We had the chance to have a regime change right here at home, when we could have denied President George W. Bush a second term, but we failed to do so (or rather, the President succeeded in winning another term, this time without a controversial Supreme Court decision). It helps us very little to claim as Senator Hilary Clinton did at a recent Democratic Presidential candidate debate, that this is the "President's war", especially when the Senator herself voted for the use of force resolution. This is the kind of dishonest political posturing that clouds our own responsibility for what an unpopular President decides. We all must take a certain amount of ownership for what is happening now, because regardless of who the President is, and regardless as to whether we are opposed to his policies, the war *is* happening in our name; the war *is* being prosecuted by our country.

* * *

The Philosophy of Anything

I began writing this chapter thinking that I wanted to talk about war in general, as opposed to specific wars in particular. But I had the inspiration to write about war in general because a theoretical discussion of war misses the all too relevant fact that at the time of my writing this book, the United States, "my" country, has been in Iraq for more than four years, and as far as polls and popular sentiment shows, the American people are sick of it. We are sick of being in the middle of a civil war that if we did not create, at the very least we helped to perpetrate by the truly precipitous overthrow of the Hussein regime, and the poorly planned aftermath of its being deposed.

Yet, when the call to military action was being voiced, there were still some people who thought that it was worthwhile to question the reasons we were being given as to why war on Iraq was a good policy. The boiled down formula to go to war went like this: Saddam Hussein is a threat to the United States, because he possesses biological and chemical weapons, and has a nuclear weapons program that will eventually give him a nuclear arsenal. Saddam Hussein's regime is furthermore a threat to the United States because it is secretly in contact with and allied to Al-Qaeda. Finally, Saddam Hussein is an evil dictator, an enemy of the United States, who kills and tortures his own people, and will stop at nothing to hurt the United States.

The White House tried to persuade Congress, the American public, and the international community at large to believe these reasons as being true. If they were, very few people I think would disagree to go to war with Iraq. But the formula, however it might have been argumentatively valid, was woefully unsound. In other words, although debatable, *if* the reasons to go to war with Iraq had been true *then* the conclusion to go to war with Iraq must have been true. Except of course, that the reasons to go to war with Iraq were not true at all. Yes, it is reasonable to believe that Saddam wished the United States harm, and yes he was an "evil dictator", but did he threaten the United States with an advanced or even rudimentary nuclear weapons program? Was he allied with Al-Qaeda? The answers to these questions are unequivocally "no". Therefore, the argument that was presented to the world to go to war with Iraq *was false*, even if it was successful in convincing some that war was the answer.

Of course, we now know that the President's policy and his unsound argument for that policy, Congress's approval of that policy and their belief in the argument for it, and our own acquiescence to the policy and the argument, has had disastrous consequences: The emergence of terrorism where before there was calm, even if it was a calm maintained by a totalitarian dictatorship; the destabilization of the entire region, whereby Iran has emerged on top in a lopsided balance of power; the squandering of world support in the wake of 9/11 by poorly planned, insufficiently invested, and foresight-lacking war-making; the deaths of innocent Iraqis by the tens of thousands, and the very significant loss of American life and treasure.

What makes war so significant for Americans right now is not just the general questions of the justice or injustice of people killing people, or the debate between war's natural or artificial causes, or the question of ideologies being contested, or what national security means in a world where terrorists are constantly

The Philosophy of Anything

on the attack. What makes this topic so significant now is not any of the just or unjust actions that are debated when it comes to discussing warfare, but the fact that these ideas are not mere ideas at the moment. Our soldiers are on Iraqi soil right now, they are being killed, and are killing, all in the name of what? All for what? All to what end? You fill in the blank. Is it for democracy? To fight terrorism? To help the Iraqis? To "defeat" Al-Qaeda in a country where they did not exist before our occupation? Now that the argument to go to war is seen to have been false, what arguments are raised to *stay* at war? Even if we entertain those arguments, should we just ignore, as some people suggest we do, the fact that we went to war for reasons that proved to be false?

When the United States went to war in Afghanistan after the terrorist attacks of 9/11, we had an almost indisputable and clear-cut case of a terrorist organization being harbored by an illegitimate governmental regime. Did we go into Afghanistan to liberate the Afghani people? No. We went in to retaliate against Al-Qaeda and the Taliban; we went in to get Osama bin Laden. Before we invaded Iraq, did we succeed in that task in Afghanistan? By no means. We are still losing troops in, and losing the battle for Afghanistan, in an operation that has been overlooked by the public and by the administration, in favor of a war that never needed to happen. In 2001 we went to war with the almost unanimous support of the world. In 2003 we stood with very few friends in the desert, and now, in 2007, the Afghani conflict is not being prosecuted to a sufficient or successful extent, and Iraq is a different sort of nightmare than it was when Saddam ruled.

And Iraq and Afghanistan are of course by no means the only places where the American military presence is felt: scores of other locations see our troops in harms way, resulting from a White House that seems intent on escalating conflict where it might, and resisting conflict where it should quickly respond. I have in mind specifically the Darfur region of Sudan, where a Sudanese government stands impotently and perhaps complicitly by while the genocide of its own people is perpetrated by elements that for very good reasons should be labeled "terrorist", and yet the United States and the international community still patiently entertains the Sudanese position to not allow foreign peacekeepers to establish order, even while we oppose that position. What about regime change in Sudan? What about a military policing engagement that would require comparatively so few troops and such minimal treasure, and that could be so beneficial to those who are affected by the emergency? What about stopping unjust killing for something other than a sphere of influence? Shouldn't we ask ourselves where our priorities lie, and whether a conflict that is necessary has been abandoned for a conflict that is unnecessary?

However much war could be discussed in general, then, what makes it relevant now, for Americans, is our involvement in this war, in Iraq and Afghanistan, and in the inappropriately and ironically terrifying named "war on terror". I have the disheartening, pessimistic, and some would call "unpatriotic" position that we are losing both wars, but I also feel that we need not continue on this path. We are losing in Afghanistan because we have not committed ourselves to winning with the resources and national will that it is necessary and possible for us to commit. We are losing in the failed democratic state of Iraq because it was an impossible situation to begin with, and because we feel compelled to fight a counterinsurgency, that despite its threat, we and the Iraqis do not yet know how to overcome. How to think critically about these issues, and how to resolve the troubling state of affairs we see in real and current events? Can we find a solution by trying to think critically about the dilemma our country has placed itself in?

* * *

As I think about what more to write concerning war, and when I look over what many will see as a editorialized polemic against the President and his policy concerning Iraq, I wonder if we can view this circumstance, and my articulation of what I see as a misguided and miscalculated war, as a platform to begin thinking, and to contemplate what war means in general, and what it means at this moment in history?

I also wonder if my very strong feelings on the subject illustrate just how difficult it is to think critically about an issue that hits so close to home. Here is an issue that it is very challenging for me to be non-committal about, since I care so deeply about it. Even for someone who is supposed to have something to offer others in terms of how to accomplish thinking, I still find myself plagued by uncompromising positions, and what at times is a black and white view of an issue that really matters to me, and that has so many shades of gray that I find myself wondering whether I might not be mistaken.

Since war really matters to so many people, though, and since today, our current war is so controversial, I need to remind myself that my view on the situation is not infallible. So many people I know and whose opinions I take seriously, some of my own family members included, have different perspectives on this subject, and I'd like to think I am open to what they think, and to anyone's differing thoughts, even if the substance of those thoughts frustrates me.

Also, when I try and examine the reasons that support my beliefs and my judgments, I come to realize that those reasons need reasons themselves, and I'm left feeling that to provide enough support for why I feel the way I do is an insurmountable task. Why, then, should I expect anyone else to clear that highly set hurdle for proof? Perhaps I can be sympathetic to their perspectives, knowing that my own is not immune to criticism, and learning something from another's point of view.

But when we're talking about war, and when we're talking about the war in Iraq, I want to somehow give credence to my strong emotions, and the gut feelings that I have. And at the same time I want to strive to understand, even if my feelings tell me that I already do. Again, the challenge to thinking is that we care so much about what we think, and that what we think is who we are. Thinking about war tells us something about ourselves. The challenge with this issue as with so many others, is to reach beyond who we are, for the truth and for understanding, even in the face of apparent certainty.

Conclusion:

The Critical Thinker after Graduation

Whatever you decide to do after graduation, you will continue to be confronted with situations that require you to make choices, and circumstances that will test your ability to think critically about issues that have an impact on your life. Your beliefs will be called into question, and your reasons for why you hold those beliefs will be doubted, by yourself and by others. People will wonder whether you've thought things through, and whether you really know what you claim to know. You'll ask yourself if you're sure, and many times, even if you admit that you are not, you will still have to choose to act. You're certainty regarding things that are important to you will continue to be challenged, by others and by yourself, when you are faced with conflicting ideas, and no clear path.

If one thing is certain, it is that there will be moments in your life when you are uncertain, when an answer is not forthcoming, and when even the question is hard to articulate. It will then take courage for you to think, and to act. It will take effort for you to choose.

And your education will not end once you walk down the aisle, shake hands with the Dean, and receive your diploma. Nor will it end if you decide to skip class all the time, or drop out of college altogether. And even if you never go on to Graduate school, your education will continue. Your education, in other words, is unavoidable, and unending. The question is, what will your education consist of? What you will learn, how seriously will you take that learning, and how receptive will you be to lessening your own ignorance, and charitably entertaining new thoughts and new ideas, once you have left the environment that is specifically designed with these sorts of things in mind?

Let's say you get a job. Then you'll have to learn the details of your job duties, the special skills that will allow you to do what's expected of you in the context of whatever work environment you are in. You'll have to learn how to cooperate with your coworkers, and your bosses; the workplace, after all, is a political environment. And you'll have to learn how to balance your job duties with your personal life, so that one does not come too much at the expense of the other.

Let's say you deicide to have children. Then you'll have to figure out the hardest thing in the world: learning how to educate and raise and nurture another person who depends upon you entirely. If you're not a single parent, you'll have to learn how to live with your spouse and continue to have a meaningful and healthy relationship in the face of your job, your child, and everything else in your life. Also, let's not forget this very complicated, very scary world that we live in today, with the threat of terrorism, a government that needs to be constantly persuaded that our individual rights are worth protecting, and a society in which intolerance has prevented a just provision of equality among all its citizens. How to learn to live in a world like this, and how to raise children in this environment?

When your formal education ends, your informal education will continue. It will continue as it has continued throughout your life, since before you began your long journey through the institution of formalized education. When you no longer have books that are assigned to you, there will still be so many books left to read, and simply not enough time to read them all. When the events of your life stop revolving around classes, and final papers, and tests, you'll still have obligations to meet, and you'll still be evaluated according to how much effort you put into fulfilling those obligations. When questions arise, as they inevitably do, they will still need to be confronted with intelligence and thoughtfulness if you are to make sense of them, and if you are to understand how they might be answered.

Today we are confronted with only one moment in our lives. We can use this moment to chose to think about where we stand, and why we stand where we do, or we can turn on the television, and watch something other than the news. We can try to be aware of the world around us, and the reasons in our own heads, or we can get so distracted by the world and our own day-to-day lives that thinking becomes more often than not the neglected choice. Today we are confronted with only one moment in our lives. How many more moments will there be to become a more thoughtful, engaged person? How many more opportunities do we have to be the most informed, passionate, and reasonable people it is possible for us to be?

Our time, to one degree or another, is limited. So we must take the opportunity to think as it presents itself to us, now. We can only hope to accomplish thought if we take the time to think. We can daydream all we want, but this is not thinking. Thinking occurs when we take things one step at a time, and when we recognize hard questions when we are confronted by them. Thinking occurs when our opinions are flexible enough to encounter reason in a constructive way. Thinking occurs when we direct our intellectual energy towards objectives that matter.

If this book has accomplished anything, I hope it has inspired you to think. I hope that those who have read it, and who wish to reject anything I have said, can argue for *why* they reject what they do. Similarly, I hope those who are sympathetic to my thoughts can think for themselves, and decide why what I have written rings true, or makes sense to them. Finally, I hope that opposing perspectives, no matter what their substance, or context, can be understood by the people on either side who hold them.

The greatest challenge to thinking is ourselves. We feel so strongly about so many important things, that these strong feelings become a part of who we are. We resist thought because to think is to expose ourselves to the world and to others who

The Philosophy of Anything

might disagree. Then we are confronted with the prospect of trying to understand why we feel the way we do, and why we are who we are, and this confrontation challenges us, and strikes us to the core. When we think about who we are, and what we believe, and when we inquire into the things that matter to us, we have a chance to grow into an individuality that is more than just taste or opinion, more than just how we feel. When we begin to think, we begin to think about ourselves, examining our lives and making them worth living. After graduation, we can continue to grow as thinkers, knowing ourselves better so we can begin to better know the world.

Appendix A:

Student Essays

At the beginning of every semester, usually on the first or second day of class, I assign to my students what I consider to be a very meaningful piece of homework. The freshmen who are enrolled in the section of *Introduction to Critical Thinking* that I teach at San Francisco State University are usually not too thrilled at the prospect of doing a bit of writing so early on in the semester. Knowing this full well, I nevertheless tell them I want to diagnose their composition skills, and their ability to think. I tell them they'll be graded "credit/no credit", according to their grammar, proofreading, and clarity of prose. As I try to look them unflinchingly in the eyes, I ask them to give me one page of double spaced text, addressing the prompt, "What's the Point?".

Usually, I'm met with exasperated looks and even more exasperated vocalizations when my students realize that that's all the direction they're going to get for this particular assignment. "What's the point of *what?*" they always ask, incredulously. "Exactly," I pointedly reply. More sneers, blank looks, and raised eyebrows. But despite the vagueness and frustrating ambiguity of the assignment, my students almost always end up impressing me with their thoughts.

This appendix consists of some of those thoughts. I include them here because I think it is instructive for people who are being encouraged to think to be allowed to see the efforts of others who grapple with thinking. Furthermore, I think my students have given some very provocative responses that are of interest not only to other students in critical thinking or philosophy courses, but also to anyone who might be reading this book in an effort to expose themselves to thinking, as it can sometimes occur intuitively, organically, naturally, without detailed instruction, and within a framework of familiar wonderment.

By the time you're 18 years old, you've probably questioned the meaningfulness of one thing or another, in your life or in the world. You've probably been baffled by something a politician said, or something you saw on the news, regarding some controversial issue. On a more mundane, but no less relevant level, when you go to college, you've got to wonder what the point of all those required courses are; the fact that *Introduction to Critical Thinking* is one of those requirements for all incoming freshmen at SFSU suggests to me that many of the students who

The Philosophy of Anything

are enrolled in that class are asking themselves why they have to be there in the first place. What's the point of having to take *Introduction to Critical Thinking*, and what's the point of Philosophy? This is one way for students to approach the prompt I give them. I want them to confront questions like these, but to do so without any specific guidance, in order to get them to explore a meaningful question that can be asked of anything and placed in any context; the only real requirement is that they find that context on their own.

As a final remark, here is a story from last semester: One of my students went to her English instructor after I gave her this assignment, (understandably) bemoaning the fact that I wasn't more explicit about what I wanted from her. Her Professor responded much like my students do when he heard the "details" of the assignment: "How does he expect you to do *that*?" he asked, I'm sure with a certain amount of chagrin. My answer, to him and to my students who invariably wonder the same, is: "By thinking. By engaging the question. By independently and creatively discovering what it means *to you*." This is *part of* what it means to be a thinking person, after all. What follows is what happens when we are willing to try to engage ourselves in intellectual discovery, when our hands are not held, and when our thinking begins.

Thank you to all my students who contributed, and who were willing to try to think.

* * *

Brianna

What is the point of going to college? Well, I guess I would have to say that the point of college is to get a good job, which leads to making more money, which leads to being successful, right? Wrong. I think that the next question is what is success. Success to me is being happy in whatever you are doing. If you are a stay-at-home-mom and you have found peace and happiness staying at home, taking care of your children, then you are successful. If you are running a large company and you love what you do, to me you are successful. Success is what you make of it. What is the point of life? I really don't know. I don't know what I'm doing here on earth yet. I think that each person has a meaning in life and I hope that everyone figures it out. There are people who have a certain talent but they hide it or choose not to show it for some reason or another. The people who choose to hide their talent may never really know their meaning in life if they continue to hide it. I wish that I had a talent that I knew about. I don't know what my talents are yet or maybe I don't have any. I'm guessing I have some sort of talent because I believe that everyone has talent in something. What is the point of war? I know that that was a big change of topic but it was the next thing that crossed my mind. I really don't know the answer to that question either but I know that I don't like it. Hell, what's the point of anything? Is there a logical answer? Who knows, all I know is that I am here to learn and I'm enjoying it so far. Hopefully this semester will be as good as the last.

The Philosophy of Anything

Gerald

"What's the point" is a broad subject and could mean multiple things. The point of doing this paper is to get us to think outside of the box. By the end of the class you had me wondering how was I going to answer this question. I believe that you are testing us to see if we can make a point. You are also trying to see if we can develop the question and explain it thoroughly, or randomly talk about it. We can either stretch this paper out to a page with something interesting to say, or we can just pretend we are writing clearly about a point that is actually unclear. The whole point is to be learning. The whole point of people trying to learn something new is so that they are able to use it in the future. We start off with learning something small to end up with a bigger understanding of the whole point of doing it in the first place. For example, we learned the alphabet when we were younger so later in the future we can use it to spell, read, and write. The whole point of going to school is to get a good education and then we can later on find a high paying job to support ourselves. We also learn lessons that make good points like if you do not succeed the first time just try and try again until you do. To make an excellent argument we will need a well-thought out point. Everything has a point to it because there is a reason why we did it in the first place. If I made a good point that the whole paper was about learning then I think I did a great job, otherwise I was just rambling on without a clear point. I wish I could go on and talk more about the point but this is the point where I stop because I have nothing more to say.

Sherry

What's the point of getting an education, more specifically a higher education? Ask anyone this question and they'll most likely cite several different reasons: it prepares you for a career; a college graduate has a chance at a better job; it is a chance to gain more knowledge about life and the world around us.

The need for higher education has become increasingly important because more people are striving to acquire more than what they already have socially and financially. Graduates have more opportunities than those who only graduated from high school, increasing their earning potential and making them more desirable in the job market.

But college is more than just job training. Although it may very well be the most common reason why people go to college, it is not the only one and it shouldn't be the only one. College is supposed to encourage people to think and to ask questions about the world and about themselves. It is supposed to stimulate their minds and encourage them to explore new ideas and to be open to gaining knowledge. Students develop life skills that will help them in every aspect of their lives, not just in their academic pursuits. The reason why most universities require general education is essentially to educate people and turn them into well informed and productive members of our society.

So what's the point of going to college? It could potentially improve your quality of life by increasing your chances of getting a high paying job and you'll learn life skills that are crucial for success.

The Philosophy of Anything

Maeve

The point of this critical thinking class is to learn ways we can study and understand material easily. The point is to be thinking about different ways to do things. There are many ways to think and the point is to think and respond creatively to any question that is given. The point is to make clear and reasonable arguments for a side that I feel strongly about. The point is to understand all sides of the argument and not be one-sided like I usually am. I hope to clearly make my points throughout the semester while using the ideas in the course readers to fully develop my statements. The main point is making sure that I attend class regularly, do all the work, study, and participate actively in class knowing that by doing this I can maintain a good grade and standing with my teacher. The point is, when I get to a word that I do not fully understand to write it down and learn the definition. The point is to make sure that our class gets enough information so that we do not keep repeating ourselves, and to think of other ways to get our points across. The point is to think in many different ways and see things from every possible angle, with the many different solutions to problems that are out there. The point is to enjoy ourselves and just start to think. I think there are many different points that can be made and many ways to look at these situations but all we need to do is be open. That is the point, the point of this class and the point of life: to be open to ideas that you might not have thought of. There is always room to expand your knowledge and all you need to do is try. That is the point.

Catherine

What's the point of these big corporations such as Starbucks? They are entirely taking out the little mom and pop shops that used to be around. These corporations don't care what they do as long as they are making money and are number one. They end up controlling the market and making small businesses go under. For the most part companies like Starbucks don't care as long as they are making money. But even though they are such a big company and they are making the mom and pop shops close they do offer their employees great benefits. Every employee is given the title partner because everyone makes up the company as a whole. They are offered medical, dental and vision within the first six months of working there. They are also offered many discounts at various places such as car rentals, hotels, restaurants and air fare. But because of all these benefits to their employees, they are drawing in the employees from the mom and pop shops, which are making those smaller businesses close even faster.

The bottom line is that Starbucks is a money hungry corporation that doesn't care about anything but growth. Starbucks has multiplied so much that in many cities, San Francisco being one of them, they are no longer allowed to expand. All in all, Starbucks is just like any other big corporation that likes and wants money, and is willing to climb over all the little people to get to where they are now. Soon these big corporations will own everything, and everything will be known as a Starbucks.

Eric

What's the point? The point is for you to get a glimpse of my writing ability and figure out a little bit about me. When this topic was assigned it was clear to me that you wanted to know a little bit about all of us before we started this class together. Some people may not write anything significant about themselves at all and that's fine too… I think. However, if I'm going to write about something, I'm not going to sit here and debate about what the point is, I'm simply going to write. Whatever comes to mind is what I'll write. I'm a freshman at San Francisco State and I love it. I've grown up in San Diego my whole life and had a wonderful childhood and early teen years. As I start my second semester of college I couldn't be any happier. I don't believe in karma and don't believe everything happens for a reason. I believe that every person has control over their life and what happens to them. You make decisions every day that affect your life. There's no outside force or being and the decisions you make you live with. Therefore, the reason I am here today is that I worked hard in high school to get the grades I needed to be accepted into SFSU. I was not born destined to come to this school and take this philosophy class. I was accepted to SFSU and then I chose the classes I would take. There is no God to give you the teachers you want and certainly no karma to make you slip on a banana peel, walking to class. I love the earth. I love anything and everything about the earth, from plate tectonics to glaciers. I haven't decided if I want to be an old humble geology professor or a stern democrat politician who saves the world from global warming.

Gizabel

What's the point? The 'point' is a dot. A dot that isn't defined because everybody should already know what the point is. The point is to finish the general education requirements in order to start working with what you love. That's what student's points should be. The point to writing this paper is to also understand that the 'point' doesn't need to be defined. It can stay somewhat of a mystery so you can think of what your particular point is everyday. A simple 'I don't know' as an answer is ok and that is the main point that everybody should understand. It's ok not to know what the point is as long as you don't forget that you have a point and later on in life you will know what that point is.

Of course, it's fine to have mini-points for everyday. An example of a mini point can be, for instance, writing that psychology report and actually thinking about it. That's something that can be accomplished and doesn't need to be dwelled upon much after. Thinking about the 'point' without knowing what the point is for, is extremely confusing. It is confusing because what if the point that you are thinking about now is totally different from the one that really is?

Teresa

Students enrolled in this class probably don't realize its benefits beyond the general education requirement. If this course was optional, many students would wonder, "What's the point?" and opt out. Goal-oriented students whose top priority is to get the most practical degree in the least amount of time are generally not interested in philosophy. But a basic philosophy course is not about learning the antiquated philosophies of the long-deceased; rather, it's categorized under Critical Thinking, and focuses mainly on the mechanics of forming logical, cogent arguments.

The ability to effectively argue a point is vital not only for school, but for almost every career imaginable. College students know that every class requires writing papers. These papers usually have a thesis which a student must prove. To prove a thesis, a student must know how to put forth logical arguments. The stronger a point comes across to the professor, the better chance a student has of earning a good grade. Badly organized essays or those that contain logical fallacies cloud a student's argument, no matter how obvious the thesis might otherwise be. These skills are essential even after graduation. Someone who has studied basic philosophy will likely be better at convincing clients or customers, drafting proposals, or recognizing the fallacies of an opposing argument. These skills can bring one far in life.

The point of this class is not just to fulfill a general education requirement. The point is to improve logical reasoning abilities, because the skills being taught in this class are essential not only for school, but for life as well.

Luciana

I often think about the point of the things I spend a lot of my time doing. I sit as the vice chair of the San Francisco Youth Commission. As I speak at a Board of Education meeting and advocate for money to be allocated for violence prevention, or while I am trying to convince supervisors at City Hall to offer a discounted MUNI pass for youth, I realize that even though I can convince one person to agree with me, or vote for what I think is right, it is still true that this system of government does not allow for quick change. Everything takes time. For an idea to become an actual law it goes through so many processes that by the time it gets voted on that same idea has gotten lost in the midst of it all, and the ballot illustrates something completely different. So I ask myself, 'What's the point?' What's the point of fighting for change that needs to happen today, if in reality anything I do now will only create an impact months, or even years, from now? What's the point of putting so much time into an issue when I know that by the time it's taken care of something else will be happening?

Violence, drugs, gangs, homelessness, education issues, jail time and probation, are only a few of the problems youth face in today's society. People say over and over that "Today's kids are tomorrow's future", but few are trying to shape the future through the youth. And that is exactly the point. If I can't do something today that will impact the future, then I have no right to complain 20 years from now when the world is even more violent, poverty-stricken, and desperate for an even bigger amount of change.

104

Brian

Many people living in our society feel that everything in their life must have an important and explicit "point". After all, who has time to watch those re-runs of "The Office" or take a stroll in the park? Neither activity seems to have any special benefit. One might be working to make money, or studying to get better grades. Many people seem to believe that all there is to life is their job and making money, or school and getting good grades. I believe, however, that these individuals are indeed missing out on the real point, which is to be happy, to have fun, and to pursue one's interests and dreams.

The road to this point isn't necessarily an easy one. It is all too easy to get caught up measuring one's success by the amount of money one makes, or the number of A's received in a semester. I find, however, that the greatest measures for success lie more in the categories of "volume of laughter per day" and "number of new or old hobbies discovered/explored." Based on observations of my dad and other adults in salary-paying jobs, the US work force tends to lean towards working more and longer hours to increase their income. It is also my experience that taking more time off from work leads to increased well-being and happiness. For example, I find that whenever my dad spends more time on leisure activities, he generally is in a better mood. I think that if our busy society would only take a little time off now and then to have fun and pursue leisure activities, we would be one step closer to achieving the "point", and one step closer to a happier and safer world.

Hue

In society today, we frequently hear that three-word question, "What's the point?", referring to just about anything one can think of. To name two, there are, "What's the point of learning math when I'm a writer?" and even, "What's the point of life?"

In addition to questioning the point of so many things, there are also many different answers to each question. Regarding the writer's question on the point of learning math, an economist may answer that math skills are necessary for a writer to foretell how much a literary work will make in a month, and whether or not the work is worth the amount of time to create. Meanwhile, a philosopher may respond that math skills are necessary for a writer to acquire logical reasoning and organizational skills for writing essays or articles. Another person may also argue that math is not only for those who will devote their careers to it, but for everyone. It is not the actual math problem that everyone will use, but the skills needed to solve the problem that everyone needs in life: skills such as searching, figuring out, and logically reasoning. These are only a few examples of the many possible answers to the writer's concern.

Sharrol

What's the point of life? Everyone has a different life, so the question will have many different answers, whether it is to make the world a better place, to spread the family name, or to make lots of money. By now, you are probably even thinking, "What's the point of this paper?", and similar to other what's-the-point questions, there are many likely answers, and each comes from a different perspective. Therefore, the question is not, "What's the point?", but rather "Which point should *I* consider?"

Life is a journey: we have our good days and our bad days. Living our lives isn't easy: we go through life with obstacles and might encounter some big catastrophes in our lives at some point. Since life is precious and too short we should live it to the fullest, because the point of just living your life is to enjoy it while you can. You can't just dwell on what's negative in your life; you should focus on the positive aspects of your life more than the negative. Don't get all depressed for a long period of time if you are dying or have a long-term illness because you should enjoy whatever time you have left. Life can't just have the positive sides to it, because there will always be the negative aspects of life as well. I don't know why, but that's just the way it is. This is how I see the point of life; some people may see it differently, but that's their way of looking at life. Interacting in activities that have positive outcomes is also healthy and surrounding yourself in a healthy environment will keep you happy throughout your life, even though happiness isn't guaranteed in life. We should try to stay happy as much as possible throughout our lives.

Janelle

By definition, a "point" is: 1) A sharp or tapered end, 2) A slight projection, or 3) A stage or condition reached. (*The American Heritage® Stedman's Medical Dictionary, Dictionary.com*). When asked to answer the question "What is the point?" I would first need to determine which definition of "point" I would use to answer this broad question. The question "What is the point?" is most commonly asked while listening to a story, or watching a demonstration; therefore to answer the question, I would use the third definition, which describes more definitely the purpose rather than a peak or spot.

Now that I have chosen which definition I will use, I must choose a story or demonstration concerning which I will define the point, or purpose. Upon attending the first meeting of our Critical Thinking class, I was skeptical that the class would be aimed toward writing and the meaning of words. After some thought about the structure of the class, I recalled that the class is mandatory. While understanding that it is required for a reason, I utilized the information given to hypothesize that the purpose, or point of this class, is not to bore students, but rather to strengthen vocabulary and expand our way of thought. Given this first assignment, each student was expected to test his or her interpretation of the prompt. The broad and confusing prompt is a great demonstration of how the class will operate. To analyze a situation and to understand the meaning of that situation is what I believe to be the point of this assignment.

Mike

Throughout my education there has always been one question standing in my way of learning. The question simply is: "What's the point?" This question stands in the way of people learning something new and useful. If people just accepted some of the knowledge that is given to them, they might find themselves a lot happier.

In high school, the question, "What's the point?" arose quite frequently. People were always asking, "Why do we have to do this? I ain't gonna be no mathematician." I guess in the eyes of the great philosopher Socrates, it would be a good thing to have people asking all these questions. But when we start letting this stand in the way of the education that teachers are trying to offer us, it stops being simply inquisitive and it starts to handicap us. Kids wonder why we have to learn weird words. The answer is to simply expand our minds, and to have a better vocabulary. Sometimes my peers would complain and say they are not going to live in Mexico or Spain ever and that they shouldn't have to learn such a stupid language such as Spanish. Do they even have a clue as to how many people in the business world and in California speak Spanish as their first language? This kind of ignorance makes me cringe when I hear it from my peers. The fact that they can't see where we live and the countries that border us, and the huge influence different countries make on our society, makes me almost angry. This is why the question, " What's the point?" is harmful to a student's learning process, and it would be most beneficial if people could just be accepting of these things.

Kai

On the first day of class, an average student would not expect to be asked the question, "What's the point?" Therefore, when the rare instance does occur, the questioning professor will probably receive answers extraordinarily diverse in content. This being so, here is my take on the question you have put before me.

The course syllabus states that the goals of this class are to "develop and strengthen skills involved in understanding, criticizing, and constructing arguments—providing foundation for further work not only in philosophy but in other fields as well." Since I view "goals" and "points" as having a similar meaning in this context, I think the "point" of this course is synonymous with this defined goal.

The defined purpose of this course, however, is not necessarily everyone's reason for taking it. Many students are enrolled because it's a general education requirement, but while that influenced my decision in enrolling, it was not the only deciding factor. My reason for enrolling in your class is equivalent to the syllabus definition. My goal, point, or reason, for taking this course is to improve my argumentative skills. As a headstrong, cocky political science major, what more could I wish to gain from a course than to argue more effectively? Money, networking, and false promises may get someone into public office, but the ability to convince and argue effectively can be a much more powerful vehicle for getting things accomplished. That is what I am here for, and that is what I hope to gain from your instruction throughout the semester. That is the point.

The Philosophy of Anything

Shawn

I believe that making choices is the point of everything. Everything you do requires you to make a choice. If people know themselves really well then they are more likely to make a choice that is best for them.

I think the point of going to college is to get a good degree in something you enjoy doing so it will be easier for you to get the job you want and you'll be paid more for it. I also believe that the social impact the dorms have on students are equally as important. Another point of living in the dorms is for students to learn more about themselves through the relationships that they have with the people around them. Living in the dorms forces you to get to know yourself better than you ever have before.

Most people don't see this side of what college is going to be like when they are thinking about going to school, so they decide to not go. I think those people are missing the point.

College tests your social abilities to see who you can deal with and for how long. It shows you what type of people you are compatible with in a relationship and a friendship. You learn more about yourself during these years than you have in all your years of schooling so far. You live on your own for the first time and are forced to make a lot of responsible decisions. You have to learn how to balance work and play. Being in college, having a job, and trying to live a social life all at the same time forces you to grow up and handle these different situations like an adult. These skills will follow and help you later on down the road. This is the point of going to college.

Brianna

Most People believe the only point of a college education is to obtain a high paying job, but realistically, the advantages of a higher education are endless. Especially as a woman, I believe that receiving a quality education is a huge privilege because many women in the world are not as fortunate. Therefore the value of my education is of far greater worth than some job after college. The point of my college education is to learn and discover as many new experiences and ideas as possible. When an individual graduates from college, they complete a chapter in their life as a well rounded intelligent person of society. The point of a college education is that it is priceless.

The point of attending college is what you get out of it, and you always get as much out of college as you put into it. Anyone who attends college at any given establishment has to pay fees and purchase expensive textbooks. The only real difference between educations received by students is the knowledge they ultimately leave with at graduation. The point of a college education is to experience as many new things as possible. People who just attend classes are not going to receive the same education as the students who attend classes in addition to sporting events, club events, and theater productions. The more real life experiences you encounter as a student the more versatile you are in the professional world. Leaving college with an education means the ability to think critically and contribute constructively as an individual to society.

Kelsey

What is the point? As individuals we ask ourselves this question everyday, regarding anything from determining if a relationship has any meaning left to the meaning of a particular activity. The question is also posed regarding our society as a whole. We ask "what is the point?" about our roles in society and even in the discussions of political ideas. So, what is the point?

Individually speaking, the point is clear. The point is to have the clarity of mind to ask this question to ourselves every morning and at every situation. If there is no questioning of our personal endeavors then these endeavors are immediately accepted. The acceptance of any situation or activity leaves our position suddenly mediocre and meaningless. To whole-heartedly accept these ideas leaves no room for interpretation or analysis. Asking questions validates and strengthens the meaning of these circumstances. Questions provide an individual with the ability to clarify the meaning and personal struggle of an event. Asking "what's the point" helps to strengthen an individual's stance.

As a society this stands true, as well. We are united as the public, and one role is to determine how to better ourselves as a whole. Strengthening the meaning of these ties, we involve ourselves by taking stances on political and humanitarian issues. As we step into these roles and produce these ideas the most fundamental step is to ask questions. And, as the individual must, societies too are required to ask what the point is. The question, along with many others, is there to bolster an opinion, or create stepping-stones of ideas. The point is to ask, "what is the point?"

Jonathan

"What is the point?" I believe that this is a very vague question that can be taken and looked at in a number of different ways. I believe that a point is very important because it is essential to understanding the main idea of an argument. Throughout my life and career as a student, I have noticed that points play a major role in causing people to believe the credibility of what a person says, whether it is an essay or persuasive speech. I have also noticed that when a person states their point, it is very important that they are able to support their argument with sub-points.

As a first-time freshman at San Francisco State University, I have had to demonstrate my ability to support a main point in a number of courses, including my English composition class and Speech class. The ability to support a main point was especially important in my Speech class because when giving a speech you have to be able to support your point to show the audience that you know what you are talking about. A point is also a key factor in writing an essay because it sets up the following paragraphs that are supposed to support the main point. While a point plays a significant role in one's academic studies, it can also play a very important role in situations where a person may need to be persuasive. For example, a person may need to address specific points about himself or herself in an interview to persuade an employer that they are right for a job. A point is also very significant in a court of law because a more plausible point can decide one's fate.

Tami

What's the point? That is a very broad question that relates and applies to many things in life. I believe this paper is to help tease our brains into thinking outside the box and to think critically as well as individually to come up with our own ideas for this paper. Therefore I got the idea to write about society and some of the different current issues surrounding us.

Cosmetic surgery is a huge issue today, and is widely advertised and encouraged among citizens by the media. What's the point? It just goes to show how superficial and artificial people can get, emphasizing more on outer beauty rather than inner beauty. Botox injections, breast augmentations, and nose jobs as are among the numerous popular plastic surgeries done and publicly glorified in the media. The media is just taking it way too far with portraying and emphasizing outer beauty.

The war with Iraq is another issue that is strongly affecting Americans and all those who have lost a loved one in the war. I understand Bush is trying to protect other countries and end the war on terrorism but we have already lost thousands of our own troops in Iraq, so what's the point of losing more innocent lives?

I have come across plenty of heartaches, from losing a family member to a drunk driver, to losing a family member to cancer. I've realized life is too short, so what's the point in trying to strive for all the hottest materialistic things in life? I have learned to not sweat the small things in life such as mishaps with my peers or family because there is no point, and there are more things in life that are worth living for.

Christopher

What is the point of increasing the cost of tuition? Higher education has become substantially more expensive from year to year and the cost of tuition continues to rapidly grow. For example, the cost of tuition at SFSU has nearly doubled since 2002. In fact Gov. Schwarzenegger has proposed to raise the cost of tuition. He plans to increase undergraduate tuition for California State Universities by 10 percent and by 7 percent for the Universities of California. The current fee for a full-time undergraduate student at SFSU is 1,583 dollars per semester, making tuition about 3,166 dollars per year. If this tuition bill is passed, that will increase tuition by 316 dollars per year. Raising tuition cost is unfair because it can cause serious consequences for thousands of financially unstable students. Adding to students' already accumulated debt is not going to encourage higher education. If the government wants a greater number of better educated citizens with college degrees, then it should stop demanding more money from students.

The government takes more money away from students than they give. In fact, the government has frequently reduced its funds for student aid and grants, making it impossible for all financially hindered students to qualify for government money. For example, the Pell Grant is given to low income students who need financial aid to attend college, but now if a person is not considered to be "poor enough" they no longer qualify for it. For students today the reduction of government money has really become a burden. What's the point of college if its not affordable?

Appendix B:
Student Essays Continued

Halfway through the semester I assign to my students the final paper for the course. Unlike the diagnostic essay, this piece of writing is longer, counts towards a student's final grade, and is not simply meant to test their composition skills. Instead, the essay is meant to give students an opportunity to voice their opinion, but to do so argumentatively. I assign the paper halfway through the course to give students an opportunity to revise and edit their work, and to do so with continuous feedback on what works and what doesn't. Included below is the assignment as they receive it, along with three exceptional essays to serve as examples of critical thinking in an argumentative mode.

FINAL PAPER TOPIC: Your Unpopular Opinion (with Arguments)

For your Final Paper in this class you will write a 5-7 page ARGUMENTATIVE essay regarding an unpopular opinion that you genuinely hold. **FIRST** you will state your opinion (your claim, or the conclusion to what will become your argument), why it is unpopular, and who it is unpopular with. You will need to be charitable in your assessment of why others do not agree with you, as later on in the paper you will analyze the potential arguments that people might use to dispute your claim (see below). **SECOND**, you will offer arguments in support of your claim. In other words, *reasons* that support your conclusions. These may consist of any of the forms of argument we studied in class (arguments by example, by analogy, from authority, about cause and effect, and deductive arguments, etc.) but you must use *at least two* of these different types of argument. Remember, if you do not justify your premises exhaustively, then your argument is significantly weakened. So make sure that you can defend the premises you use to make your conclusion. **THIRD**, once you have thoroughly argued for your position, anticipate arguments against it. In other words, *how* would people disagree with you. Note, I am not asking you to just state the opposite perspective (*that* people disagree with you) but rather *how* and *why* they do. This means you will have to *charitably* anticipate arguments from the opposite perspective, *as well as* point out the weaknesses of your own arguments in favor of your position. **FOURTH**, offer rejoinders that address the opposing arguments, and that defend your own. As a conclusion, summarize the dialectic that you have created, and rearticulate your position, and why it makes sense according to your arguments. Do not number the segments of the essay, as I have done in writing this assignment. An essay may have sections, but they all need to flow together as one piece.

I will be grading this paper on all fronts: Clarity of arguments, lack of fallacious reasoning, clarity of prose (grammar, syntax, etc.), charitableness of your presentation of the opposing perspective, etc., will all be assessed by me. In other words, *everything* counts. But a note of reassurance: Don't worry about expressing an opinion that you might think is unpopular with *me*. It is whether you do a good job *arguing* for it that matters. If you have any questions or concerns, be sure to voice them *early* and *often*. Good luck.

Sherry's Final Essay

The issue of legalizing marijuana is very contentious. The prohibition of the use, possession, and/or sale of marijuana only became illegal in the United States during the 1930s.[1] Since then, many advocacy groups have fought for marijuana law reforms to decriminalize marijuana.

In this paper, I will consider some of the arguments as to why the government should decriminalize the use and sale of medicinal marijuana. Marijuana has been proven to be an effective relaxant with few acute side effects; it is not as addictive as other "hard" drugs; it does not lead to the use of other narcotics; and the relative "harm" from the use of marijuana when compared to the use of other legal drugs does not warrant its prohibition. Furthermore, if decriminalized, marijuana could be taxed which would generate a significant revenue for the federal government.

I will present and refute the opposing claims from many medical organizations that claim that marijuana is unsafe and that the legalization of marijuana use could cause some serious health risks such as brain damage, heart disease or cancer, and furthermore that marijuana is a "gateway" drug that could lead to "harder" drug use. I will then reiterate the arguments that marijuana is beneficial and safe with moderate use, that it is not a gateway drug, and that if taxed, could generate more revenue for the government. Evidence against the use of marijuana is insufficient to warrant a prohibition on marijuana. For those

---

[1] http://www.druglibrary.org/schaffer/Library/studies/cu/cu56.html

reasons, the government should legalize medicinal marijuana use and possession for all adults.

Marijuana used as alternative medical purposes has been proven to have some positive health benefits. Many patients have used marijuana to reduce ocular pressure caused by glaucoma and to help curb nausea caused by chemotherapy, when prescribed by doctors. It is used as a muscle relaxant in spastic disorders and also as an appetite stimulant in the wasting syndrome caused by the human immunodeficiency virus infection.[2] Drobinal, a THC derived compound that is found in marijuana, is an FDA approved cannabinoid and is prescribed as an appetite stimulant primarily for HIV/AIDS, chemotherapy and gastric bypass patients. Researchers have also developed a marijuana-derived compound that could relieve pain and inflammation without the mood-altering side effects of other drugs. The compound could improve treatment of a variety of conditions, including chronic pain, arthritis and multiple sclerosis. With the development of this drug, it could potentially replace aspirin and similar drugs because of the lack of toxic side effects.

According to Jocelyn Elders, the former U.S. Surgeon General, marijuana is less toxic than many of the other drugs that physicians prescribe every day. In fact, marijuana has been used to treat nausea, vomiting and other symptoms caused by the harsh drugs used to treat certain illnesses.[3] It is a safe drug and is less detrimental than alcohol or tobacco which are legal in the United States.

---

[2] http://www.medicalmarihuana.ca/health.html
[3] http://www.maps.org/media/pj032804.html

The Philosophy of Anything

In a research paper published in the Lancet, Professor David Nutt of Britain's Bristol University and colleagues used three factors to evaluate the harm of drug use: amount of physical harm to the user, potential for addiction, and the impact on society. They determined the harm associated with any drug and comparatively ranked them. Alcohol was ranked the fifth and tobacco was ranked as the ninth most harmful drug with marijuana coming in 11th.[4] Since alcohol and tobacco are legal, marijuana should be legalized as well.

Also, unlike tobacco, according to Daniel E. Ford M.D., a researcher from Johns Hopkins Medical School, marijuana is unlikely to cause head, neck or lung cancer. Based on these findings, Ford says that cancer prevention efforts should remain focused on tobacco and alcohol, two known carcinogens.[5] Furthermore, there have been no reported deaths or permanent injuries sustained as a result of a marijuana overdose.

The war on drugs is expensive. Many resources go into catching those who buy or sell drugs on the black market. These costs seem particularly exorbitant since marijuana, as it is widely used, is no more harmful than the legal drugs such as alcohol and tobacco. The illegality of marijuana use and subsequent black market profits has attracted criminal activity. Those profits could very well have gone to the federal government. With taxation and regulation, the legalization of marijuana could generate more tax revenue for the government. In a recent study for the Fraser Institute, economist Stephen T. Easton argued that if marijuana

---

[4] http://www.msnbc.msn.com/id/17760130/
[5] http://www.webmd.com/news/20000508/marijuana-unlikely-to-cause-cancer

was legalized, excess profits and tax revenue could be transferred to the government instead of the black market criminals, many of whom have ties to wealthy organized crime syndicates. [6] Revenue from marijuana could go to the construction of new roads, health care, or other social welfare programs. A report by Jeffrey A Miron, a professor of economics at Harvard University, estimated that legalizing marijuana would save $7.7 billion per year in government expenditure on enforcement of prohibition. $5.3 billion of this savings would accrue to state and local governments, while $2.4 billion would accrue to the federal government.[7]

Despite these reasons, many opponents of marijuana legalization argue that marijuana should not be legalized because, like cigarettes, it is unhealthy and could cause lung cancer and emphysema. According to Dr. Marinel Ammenheuser from the University of Texas, marijuana smoking causes the same kind of damage to DNA as tobacco. After reviewing some studies, the American Cancer Society found that smoking marijuana contains known carcinogens and smoking delivers harmful substances and may be an important risk factor in the development of lung diseases and certain types of cancers.

Although marijuana may contain some carcinogens that could potentially cause cancer, a recent study conducted by Dr. Donald Tashkin, a pulmonologist from the David Geffen School of Medicine at the University of California-Los Angeles, found that

---

[6] http://economics.about.com/od/incometaxestaxcuts/a/marijuana.htm
[7] http://www.prohibitioncosts.org/mironreport.html

The Philosophy of Anything

there is no association between marijuana and lung cancer.[8] Another study conducted by Daniel E. Ford M.D. from Johns Hopkins Medical School in Baltimore, concluded that marijuana, unlike tobacco and alcohol, does not appear to cause head, neck, or lung cancer.[9] The American Thoracic Society conducted another study that suggested even heavy users of marijuana were found not to have any increased risk of lung cancer. Unlike heavy tobacco smokers, heavy marijuana smokers exhibit no obstruction of the lung's small airway, which is usually an indication that smokers will develop emphysema.

Another argument claims that marijuana is detrimental to the brain, i.e. damages brain cells, and therefore should not be legalized since it poses yet another health risk. Glen Hanson, D.D.S., Ph.D., Associate Director of the National Institute on Drug Abuse, stated that using marijuana changes the way the brain normally functions.[10] Nadia Solowij, PhD, psychologist in the National Drug and Alcohol Research Centre at the University of South Wales, Sydney, and the University of Wollongong, Australia, conducted a study that long-term heavy cannabis users showed impairments in memory and attention that endured beyond the period of intoxication and worsened with increasing years of regular cannabis use.[11] Studies done by two Canadian research teams refute that argument. The results from those studies suggested that marijuana actually promotes neurogenesis.

---

[8] http://www.washingtonpost.com/wp-dyn/content/article/2006/05/25/AR2006052501729_pf.html
[9] http://www.webmd.com/news/20000508/marijuana-unlikely-to-cause-cancer
[10] www.aischool.org/fcd/nida.pdf
[11] http://www.mapinc.org/drugnews/v02.n394.a08.html

Dr. Xia Zhang, Ph.D., of the University of Saskatchewan presented evidence from laboratory experiments in which rats were administered a synthetic cannabinoid. New neuronal progenitor cells proliferated and those new neurons were associated with a reduction in behavior typical of anxiety and depression. According to Dr. Keith Sharkey, Ph.D. of the University of Calgary, these new findings show that drugs that act on those cannabinoid receptors can have beneficial effects on brain and behavior. Also, in a September 2001 article in the Journal of Neuroscience, marijuana was found to be neuroprotective against excitotoxicity and is therefore beneficial for the prevention of progressive degenerative diseases like Alzheimer's disease.[12] New research shows that delta-9-tetrahydrocannabinol (THC), an active ingredient in marijuana, can prevent enzymes from accelerating the formation of "Alzheimer's plaques" (proteins that can inhibit memory and cognition) in the brain.[13]

Some opponents are against the legalization of marijuana because it can be considered a gateway drug. Supporters of this concept argue that people who use marijuana will go on to use harder drugs such as alcohol, cocaine, and heroine. According to the National Institute of Drug Abuse (NIDA), long-term studies of high school students and their patterns of drug use show that very few young people use other illegal drugs without first trying marijuana.[14] However, many recent scientific studies show that

---

[12] http://www.medpagetoday.com/Neurology/GeneralNeurology/tb/1934
[13] http://www.msnbc.msn.com/id/15145917
[14] Kandel, D.B. Stages in adolescent involvement with drugs. Science, 190:912-914, 197

marijuana use does not cause people to use hard drugs.[15] Although marijuana users could potentially move onto harder drug use, a twelve year study conducted by the University of Pittsburgh challenges that belief, stating that marijuana is not a gateway drug that predicts or leads to substance abuse. The study suggested that environmental aspects have a stronger influence on which type of substance is used. This evidence indicates that the likelihood that someone will transition to the use of harder illegal drugs is not determined by the preceding use of a particular less harmful drug like marijuana but rather by the user's individual tendencies and environmental factors.[16]

Some other opponents claim that many medical organizations are against the legalization of marijuana. Some studies published by organizations such as the American Cancer Society and the American Medical Association have stated that marijuana has not been scientifically shown to be safe or effective as medicine. [17] On the other hand, the American Public Health Association, one of the oldest, largest and most diverse organizations of public health professionals in the world, "urges the Administration and Congress to move expeditiously to make cannabis available as a legal medicine where shown to be safe and effective and to immediately allow access to therapeutic cannabis through the Investigational New Drug Program."[18] The American

---

[15] Tarter, Ralph E.; Michael Vanyukov, Levent Kirisci, Maureen Reynolds and Duncan B. Clark, M.D. (December 2006). "Predictors of Marijuana Use in Adolescents before and After Licit Drug Use: Examination of the Gateway Hypothesis". American Journal of Psychiatry 163 (12).

[16] http://www.sciencedaily.com/releases/2006/12/061204123422.htm

[17] http://www.drugwatch.org/Marijuana%20Resolution.htm

[18] http://www.medicalmarijuanaprocon.org/top10.htm

Medical Association, the largest association of medical doctors and medical students in the United States, did not argue against the legalization of marijuana but rather to keep marijuana in Schedule I of the Controlled Substances Act pending the outcome of more studies determining the effects of marijuana. The AMA also endorses a physician's right to discuss marijuana treatments with patients and that "effective care requires the free and unfettered exchange of information on treatment alternatives." In an article in the American Journal of Public Health, Kaiser Permanente, one of the nation's leading health care providers, recommended that medical guidelines regarding marijuana's prudent use should be established. Kaiser also stated that despite reasonable evidence for the efficacy of THC and marijuana as anti-emetic and anti-glaucoma agents, clinical research on potential therapeutic uses for marijuana has been difficult to accomplish in the United States.[19]

There is also the argument that marijuana can impair or suppress the immune system. According to the NIDA, animal studies have found that THC can damage the cells and tissues in the body that help protect against disease.[20] According to the American Society for Biochemistry and Molecular Biology, a group of Japanese scientists discovered that some cannabinoids can cause some white blood cells to lose their ability to migrate to the sites of infection.[21] A study by the University of California, San Francisco disproves that notion and suggested that marijuana

[19] http://www.pbs.org/wgbh/pages/frontline/shows/dope/body/mortality.html
[20] http://www.nida.nih.gov/MarijBroch/teenpg9-10.html
[21] http://www.sciencedaily.com/releases/2006/04/060426174508.htm

The Philosophy of Anything

does not appear to alter viral loads of HIV patients taking protease inhibitors.[22] Research studies citing toxic effects from marijuana on the immune system have been based on extremely high doses of THC given to laboratory animals. There is no conclusive evidence to support the argument that marijuana is detrimental to the immune system when used in therapeutic doses for humans. In fact, the use of cannabis boosts the appetite in AIDS patients, enabling them to eat a balanced diet to help nourish their immune system. The FDA approved three prescription medicines that have marijuana compounds to treat AIDS-related weight loss.[23] An article in the American Journal of Public Health stated that relatively few adverse clinical health effects from the chronic use of marijuana have been documented in humans.

In conclusion, marijuana should be decriminalized for all adults for medicinal purposes. Marijuana has many health benefits that could improve the quality of life for those suffering from illnesses and it can be utilized as a safer alternative because it is less toxic than other drugs that are prescribed. The decriminalization of marijuana could enrich the nation economically and socially by generating more tax revenue for the government, which could be used to fund other social programs such as health, welfare and education programs. If policy-makers fail to decriminalize marijuana, then this beneficial drug will continue to be sold on the black market and the fiscal benefits will go to criminals instead of programs that help the American public.

---

[22] http://pub.ucsf.edu/newsservices/releases/2004010258
[23] http://www.fda.gov/fdac/features/1997/197_aids.html

Teresa's Final Essay

The death penalty is one of the most divisive issues in the United States today. Only about a third of Americans oppose it[24], but their reasons are strong. Still, the abolition of the death penalty remains an unpopular position in the United States, especially among social conservatives. Defenders of abolition are often seen as sympathetic to society's most abhorrent criminals. Thus it remains an unpopular position.

In this paper, I argue for the abolition of the death penalty, acknowledge the opposing arguments, then rebut them. I begin by pointing out the immorality and unconstitutionality of state-sanctioned killing, its ineffectiveness as a deterrent for crime, and the unfairness of the process. I then address and refute the counterarguments: that death penalty brings justice to the murder victims and their families, that it costs less than a life-sentence, and that it should be maintained as long as the majority of the public supports it. Finally, I restate the reasons for my position and call for the abolition of the death penalty in the United States.

First, the concept of the death penalty is both immoral and unconstitutional. The Bible, arguably the most authoritative source on morality, commands in no uncertain terms: "Thou shall not kill," a sentiment shared by all major religions and many philosophies of life. This assertion is unambiguous, and includes neither footnote nor asterisk to indicate exceptions to the rule. Premeditated killing -- whether perpetrated by the individual or

---

[24] "Public Opinion and the Death Penalty." Gallup Polls. Results from May 2-5, 2006. http://www.clarkprosecutor.org/html/death/opinion.htm

The Philosophy of Anything

by the state -- is morally wrong. But those averse to religion or the concept of morality should note that our Constitution bears a similar statement, guaranteeing all humans the inalienable "right to life, liberty, and the pursuit of happiness." According to the constitution, life is a basic human right, which by definition is beyond the government's jurisdiction. Thus, every time our government sentences a person to death, it violates a human right. The death penalty, therefore, is both immoral and unconstitutional (not to mention inhumane.) Since our country makes laws based on what is generally agreed to be morally right and constitutionally sound, the state should enact a law to ban the death penalty.

Second, the death penalty is an ineffective murder deterrent. To determine the likelihood that the death penalty will deter murders, we should examine the mentality of a murderer in the midst of the act. It is reasonable to assume that if a person expects to get caught, he will not commit a murder. Since murders are committed, murderers do not expect to get caught. The murderers' unreasonable expectation indicates an inability of their to rationalize during the act, due to mental imbalance (assuming mentally balanced people do not commit murders.) Granted, they also lose the ability to accurately gauge long-term consequences during the act, and will not be swayed one way or another by the current legal state of the death penalty policy. Thus, a ban on the death penalty will not lead to an increase in murders. In fact, statistics corroborate this. The Death penalty Information Center (DPIC), an independent research group, compared states that practice capital punishment with those that don't, and found the former to have a higher homicide rates than the latter[25]. The group found similar results on the national level. The United States has higher murder rates than nations that have banned capital punishment[26]. These studies strongly suggest the death penalty is not an effective deterrent to crime. According to *The New Encyclopedia Britannica*[27], deterrence is the main argument for the death penalty. Since we've proven its ineffectiveness as a deterrent, we no longer have a strong reason to keep the death penalty.

Third, the legal process of the death penalty is unfair and unjust, especially to defendants who are poor or belong to an ethnic minority. Poorer defendants cannot afford the same quality of lawyers as those who are rich. Rich defendants like O.J. Simpson are able to hire a higher-class of lawyers, such as Johnny Cochran, while poor defendants often rely on public defenders, who are known to be less effective lawyers. In this way, justice is not applied evenly across economic lines -- the poor are more

---

[25] "The average murder rates per 100,000 population in 1999 among death penalty states was 5.5, whereas the average of murder rates among non-death penalty states was only 3.6."
Death Penalty Information Center. "Deterrence and the Death Penalty." 2007
http://deathpenaltyinfo.org/article.php?scid=12&did=167

[26] "Data released by the British Home Office reveals that the Unites States, which retains the death penalty, has a murder rate that is more than three times that of many of its European allies that have banned capital punishment. (New York Times, 11 May 2002)"
Death Penalty Information Center. "Deterrence and the Death Penalty." 2007
http://deathpenaltyinfo.org/article.php?scid=12&did=167

[27] "Capital Punishment." The New Encyclopedia Britannica, Vol.2, 15th Edition, 1998

likely to die from execution than the rich. Ethnic minorities are other victims of the unjust legal process. Minorities are often tried by all-white juries instead of the promised "jury of peers." Amnesty International, a human rights organization, found that minorities are more likely to be convicted and executed than whites[28]. Conversely, white defendants accused of killing minorities are less likely to be executed, for example, the Vincent Chin trial. In this trial, two white men pled guilty to the racially motivated fatal bludgeoning of Vincent Chin, a Chinese-American man. The court stunned the nation when it meted out a punishment – a $3000 fine and three-year probation – equivalent to a slap on the wrist. This case study, though particularly egregious, illustrates that the courts are not untouched by racism, and that whites are less likely to receive the death penalty than minorities. The legal process leading to the death penalty is riddled with injustice that leads to the executions of a disproportionate number of poor and minority people. Therefore, our country, founded on the concept of justice, should abolish the death penalty.

Those who support the death penalty claim it is a form of justice, justice being the administering of deserved punishment. If the death sentence is proven to be a deserved punishment, then the death penalty is justice. The death sentence is a punishment. Also, the severity of the punishment is usually directly proportional to the severity of the crime. Following this logic,

---

[28] Amnesty International. "Death by Discrimination: The Continuing Role of Race in Capital Cases." 24 April 2003
<http://web.amnesty.org/library/index/engramr510462003>

people who support the death penalty conclude that the most atrocious crime of all, murder, deserves the ultimate punishment, death. Therefore, the death penalty fits the definition for justice. Furthermore, when a murder is committed, those close to the victim feel an injustice has been committed. This injustice, although cannot be righted, can be matched, in an "eye for an eye" fashion. To take the life of the murderer is as close to restoring the balance of justice as one can get. Therefore, supporters of the death penalty argue that it is a necessary form of justice.

My response is that while it's true that the death penalty can be considered a form of justice, it is on a deeper level simply revenge masquerading as justice. The point of a death sentence isn't just to deny a murderer the right to life, as death penalty supporters argue. It is also intended to inflict harm and humiliation on the criminal in a vindictive spirit. The suicide rate of death row inmates is ten times the normal rate[29], and extra money and effort goes to making sure the inmates don't kill themselves. If the point of the death sentence is to take away their life, why not allow them to commit suicide? It seems what's important in practice is not that the criminal loses the right to life, but that the state succeeds in the act of killing him instead. When the family of a victim of murder gathers around a death chamber to watch and cheer the killing of their loved-ones murderer, the scene reeks more of revenge than of righteousness, which is actually the more prevalent definition of the word justice (as

---

[29] *Suicide on Death Row*, D Lester and C Tartaro, *J Forensic Sci.* 2002 Sep;47(5):1108-11.

opposed to "deserved punishment.") That is because above all, justice is about doing the right thing and following the law. We have already established that the death penalty is morally, ethically, and economically wrong. As far as lawfulness is concerned, the death penalty actually forces the government to act *unlawfully*. Death penalty supporters assert that because killing is wrong, we must punish the murderers *by murdering them*. The government, hypocritically, kills people to demonstrate that killing people is wrong. The government is committing a wrong act that is ironically sanctioned by the death penalty policy. Clearly, the death penalty is not justice.

Secondly, those who support the death penalty argue that a life sentence is costlier than a death sentence, and that the state should not waste money keeping convicted murderers alive. Prisons are obligated to keep prisoners alive for however long they stay in prison – even if they are sentenced for life. Prisoners enjoy three square meals a day, are guarded around the clock, and have access to health care. The state spends precious taxpayer dollars – an estimated $75,000 per year for a maximum security cell – to keep them alive[30]. Take into account that each prisoner may live on average 30 or 40 years in these prisons, and the costs really add up. Supporters of the death penalty claim that this money would be better spent improving the quality of life for law-abiding citizens outside of prisons. If the state executes murderers instead of imprisoning them for life, it may save a lot of money.

---

[30] Wesley Lowe. "Cost – Pro Death Penalty Page." 2 April 2007. http://www.wesleylowe.com/cp.html#cost

Therefore, supporters argue the state should keep the death penalty.

But actually, a life sentence costs considerably less than a death sentence, not the other way around. Though it's true prisoners sentenced to life use up tens of thousands of dollars per year until they die (though the $75,000 figure is arguable and on the high end) the legal process leading to the death penalty can cost up to several times more, into the millions. This is due to retrials, appeals, and personal restraint petitions common to practically all cases of death sentence. In the meantime, the criminal lives in a prison cell for years, racking up the same costs as those sentenced to life. Sometimes they die before their execution date; then the whole expensive affair would have been for naught. The execution itself – assuming they live long enough to be executed – also costs money. According to the DPIC, almost every study done on the issue found that the death penalty ends up costing more than a life sentence[31]. The notion that a life sentence costs more is a misconception at best and specious reasoning at worst.

Lastly, those who support the death penalty argue that because the majority of Americans are in favor of the death penalty, we should keep it. For decades, the polls have consistently shown that two-thirds of Americans support the death penalty. Two-thirds is a strong majority, so the overwhelming support for the death penalty is clear. Supporters

---

[31] Death Penalty Information Center, "Costs of the Death Penalty." 2007
http://www.deathpenaltyinfo.org/article.php?did=108

of the death penalty maintain that because we live in a democracy, we should respect the majority, and keep the death penalty for as long as public support is in its favor.

But majority support is not reason enough to keep the death penalty – a policy proven to be immoral, unconstitutional, ineffective, unfair, and discriminatory. It's true that we live in a democracy, and that the majority has a significant influence on public policy, but it's not true that majority support gets to dictate all our laws. Our democracy is a representative one, in which we agree to be governed by elected representatives who make our laws. This is because the majority does not always stand on the side that is right. For this reason, public support can be overridden by what executives and lawmakers feel is right. For example, slavery was popular in the pre-civil war days, but it was morally and ethically wrong, so President Lincoln abolished it. In regards to the death penalty, since it is proven to be ineffective, and have far more disadvantages than advantages, public support should have little influence.

The administration and the lawmakers should abolish the death penalty, and the public should push them to do it. The death penalty is immoral and unconstitutional. It is counterproductive. It is classist and discriminatory. It executes people who don't deserve to be executed. And it costs several times more than a life sentence. Such a useless and costly policy for the sake of vengeance is simply not worth it. Those who feel it's morally and ethically wrong should call for its abolition because the executions are sponsored by, and carried out in the names of taxpayers. Those concerned about the higher cost of death penalty as compared to life sentence should call for its abolition because this money can be going to education, health care, and jobs – which are more important to the average person than watching a stranger die in an execution chamber. The death penalty affects us all, so we must actively call for its abolition.

Kai's Final Essay

In this paper, I will argue that Clean Money Campaign Finance Reform should be instated in all California elections. I will accomplish this through various methods. First, I will demonstrate that California is in need of Clean Money Campaign Finance Reform and simultaneously establish the four premises for my argument. Second, I will argue for the soundness of each individual premise, present counter arguments, and finally, offer rebuttals to the counter arguments. Through these methods, I will produce an argument that is both deductively valid and sound, thus proving that Clean Money Campaign Finance Reform should be instated in all California elections.

Clean Money Campaign Finance Reform (CMCFR) allows for qualifying candidates choosing not to accept private donations to receive public funding, enabling them to run a competitive campaign. To qualify for public funding, a candidate must receive a specific amount of individual five dollar donations during a "qualifying" period. Once qualified, the candidate is eligible to receive funding up to a certain specified amount, determined by the office which he or she is seeking. However, if a privately funded candidate outspends a candidate financed on public funds, the publicly financed candidate is eligible to receive matching funds.

Now more than ever, California is in dire need of this system. The cost to run a campaign in California has skyrocketed over the past decade. Candidates have to pay for travel, publicity and marketing expenses, as well as staff and fundraising expenditures. What this creates is a situation in which a candidate, unless in personal possession of substantial wealth, must turn to others for large financial donations. In return for those donations, donors, often wealthy citizens or corporations, expect the candidate to support their interests, once elected into office. This presents problems on two fronts. First, candidates must appeal to their donors, placing the needs of their constituents on the back burner. Second, people from lower and middle class backgrounds usually do not have the financial networking connections that are necessary to raise enough money to run a campaign. This leaves the aforementioned demographic group under-represented and often unheard in the state capitol.

For this reason California is in need of a proven campaign finance reform system that, 1) effectively limits special interest influence over elected officials; 2) limits the detrimental effects of special interest funding; 3) allows for a more diverse palette of candidates to run for office; and 4) has been successful in other states.

CMCFR satisfies California's need for a proven approach to campaign finance reform. Implemented in several states, CMCFR has already produced flourishing results. Public funding of candidates was first implemented in Maine in 1996. By 2000, one-third of all Maine state legislators were publicly funded, having no ties to special interest funding. That percentage increased in the 2002 elections, yielding a state legislature in which 55% of office holders ran under public funds. Furthermore, 77% of Maine's State Senators were publicly funded.

CMCFR yielded positive results in Arizona as well. In 1998, Arizona voters passed the *Citizens Clean Election Act*, establishing public funding for all qualifying statewide candidates. Since 1998, the program has produced a drastic transformation of Arizona elections. In 2002, Arizona voters elected clean candidates for seven of the nine statewide offices up for election, including the office of Governor. Currently, 36% of Arizona's state legislature is composed of representatives that were elected on clean funding. Furthermore, in the 2002 election, there was a 64% increase in the number of candidates running for office, as well as a 300% increase in the number of minority candidates, over the election of 1998.

Proven successful in Arizona and Maine, there's absolutely no reason why CMCFR wouldn't deliver similar results in California. The governmental structure of Maine and Arizona are both alike to that of California's. All three states have bicameral body legislatures, as well as similar executive branches. Term limits of public officials are also alike.

Nevertheless, the counter-argument can be made that the cost to publicly fund campaigns in California would come at an exceptionally larger cost to the taxpayers, when compared to Maine and Arizona. First, California is a much larger state than Maine and Arizona. In California, there are more districts, bigger districts, and a larger state legislature. This results in more potential candidates to publicly fund and larger geographical areas that candidates must cover.

Television markets in California are also more expensive than in Maine and Arizona. Los Angeles and San Francisco both rank in the top five Nielsen Designated Market Areas (DMA's). The DMA rates the amount of households with televisions, and is a determinant in the cost of television advertising. The fact that California markets hold the 2nd (Los Angeles) and 5th (San Francisco Bay Area) spot in that ranking, makes advertising in the state much more expensive when compared to other states with CMCFR. Arizona's largest market, Phoenix, holds only the 13th largest DMA. Portland/Auburn/Omaha, Maine's largest television market is rated 74th overall. (Nielsen, 2007)

There is no doubt that campaign costs in California are more expensive than in Maine and Arizona, however, California's *entire* CMCFR system could be funded by a mere 0.2% increase in California's corporate tax, "restoring the corporate tax rate to a figure lower than it was from 1980 to 1996." (California Nurses Association, 2006) This results in funding not coming from individual tax payers or the state fund, but from corporations, the same corporations responsible for the millions of dollars poured into candidates' campaigns, in return for representation of the corporation's interests.

Every year, corporations, as well as political action committees (PAC's), unions, lobby groups, and wealthy individual citizens donate hundreds of millions of dollars to countless political candidates. The aforementioned types of organizations are called *"Special Interest Groups"* (SIG). They have a specific interest in some sector of life that is influenced by public policy; therefore, it is beneficial to the organization to protect and further their given interest via political influence. This is most often achieved through the donation of funds to candidates

The Philosophy of Anything

running for office. SIG will give money to a candidate who SIG believes will represent their interests during his or her tenancy in office. Furthermore, SIG will donate money with an unspoken understanding that the candidate's ear will be available to them when an issue of interest or concern arises, thus giving SIG a vehicle of influence.

Special interest funding creates a system which is detrimental to a candidate's constituents, since candidates have an unspoken obligation to his or her campaign donors. Once elected into office, if that candidate does not serve the interests of his donors, then most likely, the donor will cease to fund the candidate, thus making the candidate's reelection campaign much more difficult. This creates an incentive for an office holder to vote in favor of the interests of his or her donors, instead of in the interest of his or her constituents.

This voting trend can be demonstrated by articulating a few of many prevalent examples. Herb Wesson Jr., who served in the California State Assembly for District 47, received $410,700 from construction unions, his largest campaign donors. In bills where construction unions had a particular stance, Wesson Jr. voted in accordance with that stance on 47 out of 50 bills. His second biggest donor group, Native American tribes and governing units, donated $283,500. He voted in accordance with the groups' stance on 7 out of 8 bills. (Herb, 2007)

Fabian Nunez, Speaker of the California State Assembly and representative of the 46th district, received $216,557 from his biggest campaign donor group, attorneys and law firms. Nunez voted in accordance with the group's stance on 31 out of 40 bills.

His second largest donor group, state and local government employee unions, donated $125,500. Nunez voted in accordance with that group's stance 97% of the time. (Fabian, 2007)

For a final example, examine the influence of electric utilities in California politics. Electric utilities donated a total of $1,635,642 to numerous candidates in 2004. 100% of bills that the electric utilities opposed failed to pass through the state legislature. (Find an interest group, 2007) It is clear that SIG demonstrate an advantageous influence over state officials, which is disadvantageous to California's voters.

CMCFR will successfully limit the detrimental influence that SIG hold over public officials. The fact that CMCFR provides public funding to candidates means that a candidate is not reliant upon large donations from SIG. For example, California Governor Arnold Schwarzenegger spent approximately $43,900,000 in 2006 alone on campaign expenditures (Schwarzenegger, 2007). His unsuccessful opponent, Phil Angelides, doled out approximately $39,000,000 in 2006 to fund his campaign (Angelides, 2007). In order to fund such extravagant campaigns, both candidates were forced to accept numerous large donations from SIG. CMCFR creates a system in which candidates don't have to rely on wealthy organizations to fund their campaign.

Opponents of CMCFR argue that the program does not prohibit candidates from running under SIG funding, and therefore does not effectively limit special interest influence in office holders. Since candidates that opt to run a privately funded campaign are allowed to seek funding from special interests, there's nothing stopping them from turning down public funding and running a campaign on special interest donations. SIG often have deep pockets, therefore a privately funded candidate will be able to raise monumental amounts of funds, just as Angelides and Schwarzenegger did in 2006, and run a more competitive campaign than a candidate running on public funds.

This is not the case however. If a candidate running under special interest funds spends more than a publicly funded candidate, the publicly funded candidate is eligible to receive matching funds, thus enabling the publicly funded candidate to wage a competitive campaign. Furthermore, one can draw from the aforementioned percentage of "cleanly" elected candidates in states with CMCFR, that voters take kindly to the idea of a government official with no special interest ties.

Significantly, CMCFR not only limits the amount of special interest influence in office holders, but it also allows for a more racial, social, and financially diverse ballot of candidates. Campaigning for public office in the state of California is, without doubt, tremendously expensive. Under the current system, only those with hefty financial backing can competitively run for office. Therefore, candidates are most frequently from upper and upper middle class backgrounds, thus creating a government body that does not accurately reflect minority and lower class households.

In 2004, 29% of legislators were women, which make up half of the state's population. Furthermore, 22% of representatives were Latino, however Latinos make up 35% of California citizens. Asian Americans constitute 12% of California's population, yet less than 1% of the legislature is composed of Asian American representatives. Finally, only six African Americans served on the state legislature in 2004. CMCFR will make public funding available for anyone that qualifies, which enables a broader, more diverse palette of candidates to run competitive election campaigns.

An issue that public funding raises is the ability for "unqualified" candidates to run for public office on the state's dollar. Why should any random person in the state be able to receive public funding to run for office? Someone who is not qualified to run for office should not be able to do so at the expense of government funds, therefore, CMCFR could be of financial detriment to the state.

In evaluating this counterargument, one must look at the issue at hand. One of the reasons why CMCFR is effective is that it allows for a larger and more diverse ballot. Currently, the only major requirements to run for public office are to be a registered US citizen, and to be eligible to vote for the office being sought. The qualifying of candidates to run for office is not evaluated by a college degree, occupation or other means. The qualification of candidates is established by the votes cast by the candidate's peers, the people. That is why CMCFR establishes a system in which candidates must receive a large amount of five dollar donations in order to qualify for public funding. This effectively demonstrates the support shown for him or her by possible constituents, and should stand as satisfactory evidence for their qualifications to run for public office.

One must also note that, as stated earlier, the funding for this program is not coming from public taxes, but corporate taxes. The more corporations contribute to the financing of their candidates the more they are also paying, through corporate taxation, for the matching funds of the publicly funded candidates.

Throughout this paper, I have explored the arguments for and against CMCFR. I demonstrated why California is in need of a proven campaign finance reform system that effectively limits special interest influence over elected officials, limits the detrimental effects of special interest funding, allows for a more diverse palette of candidates to run for office, and has been successful in other states. Furthermore, I thoroughly argued that CMCFR satisfies all those needs, and in doing so, have proven the soundness of the aforementioned premises, and thus have presented a sound, deductively valid argument for CMCFR.

In conclusion, I shall note that the issue of campaign finance reform is a very complex topic. I believe that beyond the establishment of CMCFR, restricting the size of donations from SIG would be an effective tool in limiting the power that SIG hold over office holders. Restriction of donations, however, brings up the issue of restricting one's first amendment right, by preventing a candidate the means to say what he or she wants. This is one of several issues involved in campaign finance reform, which due to length requirements, could not be addressed in this paper. Over the course of my college career, I hope to further investigate and articulate my findings in the field of campaign finance reform, with a goal that one day I will see a successful system implemented in the great state of California.

REFERENCES

1) Arizona Clean Money. Retrieved May 10, 2007, from California Clean Money Campaign Web site:http://www.caclean.org/solution/arizona.php

2) (2007). Campaign finance: Schwarzenegger - 2006, Californians for. Retrieved May 21, 2007, from Cal-Access Web site: http://cal-access.ss.ca.gov/Campaign/Committees/Detail.aspx?id=1261585&session=2005

3) (2007). Campaign finance: Angelides 2006. Retrieved May 21, 2007, from Cal-Access Web site: http://cal-access.ss.ca.gov/Campaign/Committees/Detail.aspx?id=1253280&session=2005

4) (2007). Fabian Nunez. Retrieved May 21, 2007, from maplight.org Web site: http://www.maplight.org/map/ca/legislator/97

5) (2004). Growing Representation. Retrieved April 28th, from Asian Week
Web site: http://www.asianweek.com

6) (2007). Herb Wesson Jr.. Retrieved May 21, 2007, from maplight.org Web site: http://www.maplight.org/map/ca/legislator/114

7) (2007). Find an interest group. Retrieved May 21, 2007, from maplight.org Web site: http://www.maplight.org/map/ca/interest/browse/Energy+%2526+Natural+Resources/Electric+Utilities

8) California Nurses Association, (2006). Get the facts. Retrieved May 21, 2007, from Yes on 89 Web site: http://www.cleanmoneyelections.org/yeson89-facts.html

9) Maine Clean Money. Retrieved May 10, 2007, from California Clean Money Campaign Web site: http://www.caclean.org/solution/maine.php

10) (2007). Nielsen Reports 1.1% increase in U.S. Television Households for the 2006-2007 Season. Retrieved May 19, 2007, from Nielsen Media Research Web site: http://www.nielsenmedia.com/nc/portal/site/Public/menuitem.55dc65b4 a7d5adff3f65936147a062a0/?vgnextoid=6573d3b8b0c3d010VgnVCM1000 00ac0a260aRCRD#

Appendix C:

Suggestions for Further Reading

If you're interested in learning more about the issues that have been covered in this book, then you'll want to read other books that treat those issues in greater depth, with greater expertise, and with a more lofty goal than merely introducing you to thinking about them. This book is the result of my general acquaintance with issues and with a philosophical way of thinking, but arises intuitively out of a desire to challenge young people to think. If you want a more scholarly approach, than this list of titles and their authors will hopefully help you to increase your understanding.

* * *

Books about Philosophy and Reasoning

- Cornman, Lehrer, Pappas. *Philosophical Problems and Arguments: An Introduction,* 3rd. ed. Indianapolis: Hackett Publishing Company, Inc., 1982
- Green, Mitchell, S. *Engaging Philosophy: A Brief Introduction.* Indianapolis: Hackett Publishing Company, Inc., 2006
- Nagel, Thomas. *What Does it All Mean? A Very Short Introduction to Philosophy.* New York: Oxford University Press, 1987
- Needleman, Jacob. *The Heart of Philosophy.* San Francisco: Harper & Row Publishers, 1982
- Russell, Bertrand. *The Problems of Philosophy.* London: Oxford University Press, 1959
- Weston, Anthony. *A Rulebook for Arguments.* Indianapolis: Hackett Publishing Company, Inc., 2000

Books about Morality

- Aristotle, *Nicomachean Ethics.* Translated by Terence Irwin. Indianapolis: Hackett Publishing Company, Inc., 1999
- Hart, H.L.A., *Law, Liberty, and Morality.* Stanford, California: Stanford University Press, 1963
- Lewis, C.S., *The Screwtape Letters.* San Francisco: Harper Collins Publishers, 2001

- Melchert, Norman. *Who's to Say?* Indianapolis: Hackett Publishing Company, Inc., 1994
- Nagel, Thomas. *The Possibility of Altruism.* New Jersey: Princeton University Press, 1970
- Needleman, Jacob. *Why Can't We Be Good?* New York: Tarcher Penguin, 2007

Books about Abortion and Women's Rights

- Shapiro, Ian, ed. *Abortion: The Supreme Court Decisions, 1965-2000*, 2nd ed. Indianapolis: Hackett Publishing Company, Inc., 2001
- Bringsjord, Selmer. *Abortion: A Dialogue.* Indianapolis: Hackett Publishing Company, Inc., 1997
- Shrage, Laurie. *Abortion and Social Responsibility: Depolarizing the Debate.* Oxford and New York: Oxford University Press, 2003
- Mill, J.S. *The Subjection of Women.* New Jersey: Transaction Publishers, 2001
- Sayers, Dorothy, L., *Are Women Human?* 10th ed. Michigan: Wm. B. Eerdmans Publishing Co., 2005
- Tribe, Lawrence, H., *Abortion: The Clash of Absolutes.* 2nd ed. New York and London: W.W. Norton & Company, 1992

Books about War

- Barash, David P., ed. *Approaches to Peace: a Reader in Peace Studies*. New York and Oxford: Oxford University Press, 2000

- Ehrenreich, Barbara, *Blood Rites: Origins and History of the Passions of War*. New York: Henry Holt and Company, LLC., 1997

- Kant, Immanuel, *To Perpetual Peace: A Philosophical Sketch*. Translated by Ted Humphrey. Indianapolis: Hackett Publishing Company, Inc., 2003

- Schell, Jonathan, *The Unconquerable World*. New York: Henry Holt and Company, LLC., 2003

- Sterba, James P., ed. *Terrorism and International Justice*. New York and Oxford: Oxford University Press, 2003

- Walzer, Michael, *Just and Unjust Wars: A Moral Argument with Historical Illustrations*, 3rd ed. New York: Basic Books, 1977